JUTKA

A Holocaust Survivor's Account of
Lives Destroyed and Family Rebuilt

JUDY GONDOS JACOBS

This book is a memoir reflecting the author's present recollections of experiences over time. Its story and its words are the author's alone. Some details and characteristics may be changed, some events may be compressed, and some dialogue may be recreated.

Published by River Grove Books
Austin, TX
www.rivergrovebooks.com

Copyright © 2024 Judy Gondos Jacobs

All rights reserved.

With gratitude, the excerpt from *UMKC Today* magazine is used with permission by the University of Missouri–Kansas City, © 2016.

Thank you for purchasing an authorized edition of this book and for complying with copyright law. No part of this book may be reproduced, stored in a retrieval system, or transmitted by any means, electronic, mechanical, photocopying, recording, or otherwise, without written permission from the copyright holder.

Distributed by River Grove Books

Design and composition by Greenleaf Book Group and Mimi Bark
Cover design by Greenleaf Book Group and Mimi Bark
Cover images used under license from ©Shutterstock.com/Kittyfly

Publisher's Cataloging-in-Publication data is available.

Print ISBN: 978-1-63299-800-2

eBook ISBN: 978-1-63299-801-9

First Edition

In memory of my grandparents, my aunts and uncles, my cousins, and all the other family members who never had the chance to record their memories.

Contents

Preface   vii

1. Childhood in Hungary   1

2. Digging Deeper   17

3. A Bitter Understanding   27

4. The Nazis Arrive   43

5. A Glimmer of Hope   53

6. Bergen-Belsen   65

7. Keeping Our Minds Busy   73

8. Switzerland   87

9. Embarking toward a New Life   105

10. New Horizons   119

11. Becoming American   129

12. College Years   141

13. Family Life   149

14. Other Remembrances   165

15. The Past Recalled for Good   173

The Final Word   189

Appendix   193

    Family Photos   193

    Family Genealogy   215

    Family Members Lost to the Holocaust   221

Acknowledgments   227

About the Author   229

Preface

As in life we all must go

As I write this in 2023, the Holocaust ended 78 years ago. Nazi mass deportations, gas chambers, and crematoria no longer exist, but hatred, bigotry, bullying, distrust, and violence still plague us. Have human nature and behavior changed? I wonder. Can they change? I hope so.

How do we change human behavior? There is no substantive answer, but education seems to provide a starting point.

We have neither the knowledge nor the understanding to answer the question of why there was a Holocaust, but we can explore the environment that allowed it to happen. How and why was Hitler, with his evil and self-serving goals, able to exact such a steep penalty? Educational institutions are best equipped to provide historical perspective.

Over time, lessons learned from history can change negative, hateful feelings. Hopefully, more positive sentiments will then be transmitted to subsequent generations. As parents divest themselves of intolerance, their offspring may become more tolerant. These are just first steps but certainly steps in the right direction.

We, a rapidly declining group of Holocaust survivors, are obligated to bear witness to atrocities at the hands of the Nazis. The world must know what happened, in the hope of preventing such disastrous activities in the future. Such accountings are incomplete without descriptions of life before and after the Holocaust. What was lost before the Nazi perfidy, and how has it changed the courses of victims' lives? Such reflections and reminiscences can augment and clarify what is already known.

My goal is to highlight the lessons of this infamous and tragic time period with the hope that such atrocities will never again occur. I also hope to augment the historical record and name those responsible. Revisionists provide false accounts of Nazi atrocities often bearing scant resemblance to what really happened. Holocaust deniers insist this genocide never occurred. My firsthand testimony refutes such lies. As Elie Wiesel wrote, "To forget the victims is to kill them for a second time." We honor their memories by remembering them. And finally, I want to provide my family with an answer to the question, "Who is Judy Jacobs, and why is she the way she is?"

CHAPTER 1

Childhood in Hungary

Budapest was our home. My mother, Anna Ilona Havas, nicknamed Ilus, married my father, Bela Gondos, on August 14, 1934. I, Judit, was born on April 27, 1937. Everyone called me by my nickname, Jutka. I called my mother Anyuka, Hungarian for mother, and my father Apuka, Hungarian for father.

My early years were idyllic. Being an only child, I lacked for nothing, neither attention nor material things. Though I was cared about and cared for, our family was not child-centered. My father was a roentgenologist—what is now called a radiologist—and as the breadwinner of the family, his schedule drove our daily lives. I was part of a functioning family with productive and interesting parents.

Our apartment was large by Budapest standards in the 1940s. We had three rooms for the family. An L-shaped hallway provided access to the bathroom, storage cabinets, a big kitchen, and a small maid's room. My parents' room was the largest and served multiple functions. There were two daybeds, a wardrobe, my father's large desk, arm chairs, the dining table, and bookshelves. A glass-fronted vitrine displayed beautiful porcelain artwork and my mother's watch, a small gold timepiece with sapphires and rubies marking its face. Holding and admiring it was a real privilege.

My mother had designed all the furniture, which was custom-made as wedding gifts from her parents. The middle room, the salon, was furnished with ornate Biedermeier furniture that had belonged to my mother's grandmother. Biedermeier, the Austro-Hungarian furniture from the first half of the nineteenth century, is clean and simple by design and beautiful in the way the wood grain was emphasized instead of having gold or other metal inlays. There was a sofa, six chairs of various sizes, and an oversized cocktail table. Everything was upholstered in cherry-red wool, with needlepoint inserts on the sitting pieces and table cover. Anyuka had designed and needlepointed everything.

The room also contained our baby grand piano, which had been Anyuka's as a child and had previously belonged to her grandmother, Roza Bleuer. My mother had taken piano lessons and especially enjoyed playing "Für Elise," a piece with which Apuka and I became very familiar.

My maternal grandmother, nagymama in Hungarian, was born Iren Bleuer. She was the daughter of Mor Bleuer and Roza

Bleuer, who were first cousins. Both Mor and Roza were born in the small southeast Hungarian town of Mezőtür and were grandchildren of Samuel and Kati Bleuer, who we believe were born in Zarky, Poland. Nagymama's brothers changed their names from Bleuer to Biro to Hungarianize the names. Thus, Nagymama's three brothers were Emil, Sandor, and Erno Biro.

Anyuka had inherited a pair of elaborately adorned silver candlesticks with suspended silver Biblical figures on the sides. These became our Shabbat candlesticks. Anyuka lit candles every Friday evening. Apuka's mother, grandma Roza Gondos, had planned to give silver candlesticks to my parents as a wedding gift. Since they already had a pair, she gave them a sterling chanukiah, a Chanukah menorah. It, too, was always freshly polished and used for all eight nights of Chanukah. The Shabbat candlesticks and the chanukiah were displayed on a small shelf next to the piano.

Our telephone sat on a small table between two of the Biedermeier chairs. My mother was very fond of the telephone and spent lots of time speaking with Aunt Rozsi, who was married to my nagymama's brother Erno. Apuka frequently teased her about her long phone conversations, saying, "Ilukám, don't you have anything better to do?" The addition of "ám" at the end of my mother's nickname was a Hungarian form of endearment, as if to say "my dear Ilus."

Days began with my mother, my father, and I fully dressed for an early family breakfast. After breakfast, I was expected to entertain myself while my mother instructed the maid in her day's duties. Domestic help was cheap and plentiful, and we had a live-in maid. Anyuka supervised her very closely. We had no vacuum cleaner, and the rugs had to be beaten outside. After beating the rugs clean of the previous day's dirt and dust, the maid was instructed to strap brushes to her feet. She danced across the apartment's wooden parquet floors until they were as shiny as mirrors.

The maid cooked delicious meals served three times a day—breakfast, dinner, and supper—on white damask tablecloths. Breakfast consisted of hot coffee for my parents and milk with a taste of coffee for me. The rest of the meal was composed of rolls, croissants, or toast with butter and jam.

Dinner, our big meal of the day, was a multicourse affair. There was always soup. It could be mixed vegetable soup, pea soup, or, in warm weather, cold fruit soup. Sometimes even cherry soup. Often the main course was dumplings filled with meat or cheese. We always had a cooked vegetable and a compote of apples or other fruit. Dessert was not served at the table. Apuka rested after dinner, before he went back to his office, and the maid would bring him a heaping plate of pastries that he almost always finished. Occasionally, I was allowed to share. The afternoon pastries consisted mostly of plain cookies or nut-filled delicacies, but chocolate was his favorite. Supper was a light meal. In winter we often had baked potatoes with lots of butter, one of my favorites. Supper often was served late in order to accommodate Apuka's office hours, but I always ate at the scheduled time so that I could get to bed on time at 7:00.

Once the housecleaning was organized, mother and I were free to leave. In pleasant weather we went to Városliget, the city park, where I played outdoor games such as tag, dodgeball, and hopscotch with the other children while the mothers sat on benches and chatted. The adults were totally uninhibited about disciplining other people's children. I don't recall what I did or why, but once the mother of one of my playmates slapped my face. I was too stunned to object or cry. I ran to tell my mother, but, much to my surprise, she was unconcerned.

I was brought up to be obedient and to accept the premise that children should be seen and not heard, unless they were asked to sing "Poni Panni," a popular song about a pony. At three years old, I learned to sing it, and my parents were impressed by my exceptional singing ability. Whether I liked it or not, I had to perform the song on command, on the street, at home, in the park, or wherever we happened to be. Many years later I still remembered the song and sang it for my children when we visited Budapest.

I had nice friends with whom I played in the park, weather permitting, and some invited me to their homes. My best friend was Evi. I was a weekly guest at Evi's home. Our favorite pastime was playing house. Evi's mother allowed us freedom of the apartment, a wonderful setting for our imaginations. Bori was another good friend. Playing at Bori's house was more regulated and not nearly as fun as spending time at Evi's. Agi, our neighbor, was also a playmate. When we played in her apartment, Agi concocted sophisticated meals that always contained anchovy paste. I was too shy to admit that I hated it. Nomi Gondos, my first cousin and two years my junior, was another nearby playmate. Nomi and her family lived two floors below us in the same apartment building.

Well before I was old enough to go to school, my parents found a part-time nanny, Margit néni. I don't recall her surname. Margit was her given name, and "néni" was a general term of respect for an elder woman or aunt. Margit's dress and manner were very grandmotherly. Her full-time job was caring for three very lively boys. Two were older than I, and one was younger. Her new assignment was to include me in their daily trips to the park. At about 9:30 most weekday mornings, one of the three boys yelled, "Jutka, Jutka" from the courtyard. In our "refined" neighborhood, when you wanted to call on someone, you went to the door and knocked; proper young men did not boisterously yell out from the courtyard. The neighbors noticed but said nothing. I ran downstairs as soon as I heard the boys calling me, and we walked to the park, where we played as usual.

Though it officially became the unified city of Budapest in 1873, to this day, the west side of the Danube is known as Buda and the east side as Pest. But all of Budapest was my personal playground. In winter, my father and I went ice-skating nearly every day. In the spring and early summer, my parents and I hiked and picnicked in the Buda Hills. We traveled by streetcar from Pest to Buda, where we rode the funicular to the top of the Schwab Hegy, a small mountain popular with weekend hikers. Anyuka packed a delicious picnic, and after lunch we relaxed on blankets spread on the grass. I loved to run around in the meadows to pick flowers. That's where mother taught me to weave garlands.

My parents often arranged to meet friends on these excursions. Typically, I was the only child there, and all the adults spoiled me. By the time we returned home in the late afternoon, we were all tired, and I had trouble just staying awake.

In the evening, Anyuka and Apuka often went out. They attended Zionist organization meetings or met friends at coffee houses. The maid was expected to stay with me.

My mother's aunt and uncle, Rozsi néni and Erno bácsi ("bácsi" is a Hungarian honorific for men or for uncles), lived in Pest. Ilus and Rozsi were close friends. Rozsi, an accomplished seamstress, sometimes made clothes for my mother. We visited them often. Rozsi and Erno were my backup babysitters when the maid was unavailable. I was treated like royalty in their home. And they gave me all the candy I wanted. They were sweet, warm people, and I loved their company.

The bulk of my time was spent with my parents or whoever had been hired to look after me. I was comfortable in adult company and able to hold my own in conversation, even when I had no idea what was being discussed. The maid came with me to the park only on days when my mother had other commitments. I don't think the maid liked coming with me, because she was excluded from the group of mothers and sat by herself, waiting for me to finish playing.

Friday nights were festive at our house. During candle lighting, I imitated Anyuka in saying the bracha, the blessing. We sang "Shalom Aleichem." Apuka blessed me and recited the Kiddush. Apuka's family had always sung Shabbat songs, and we occasionally sat at the table singing long after the meal was finished. Most of the time my father sang solo because neither my mother nor I spoke or read Hebrew.

Unlike Anyuka, Apuka had been raised in an Orthodox home. He told us many stories about accompanying his father to daily minyan (the quorum of Jewish adults required for certain types of prayers) and communal cooking facilities for cholent, a Shabbat dinner staple of slowly baked meat and vegetables prepared on Fridays and cooked overnight. My mother's upbringing was very different. Her family was assimilated, which meant that strict Jewish traditions and observances were altered or superseded by the customs of the country in which they lived. Her family maintained a Jewish identity and supported Jewish institutions, but they were not religiously observant. These two opposing backgrounds resulted in compromise when my parents married. They maintained a kosher home, primarily to accommodate my father's mother, but otherwise I recall no daily observance.

When I was three or four, I once walked into my parents' room and saw a strange contraption on my father's forehead and wrist. My father was speaking, but I had no idea what he was saying. It was clear that he did not want to be disturbed, so I quickly left the room. Later I learned that the contraptions on his arm and forehead were tefillin and that he was reciting Shacharit, the morning prayers. Also called phylacteries, tefillin are little black leather boxes containing verses from the Torah written on parchment scrolls. I had neither seen tefillin before that day, nor had I been exposed to morning prayers.

Chanukah was always memorable in our home. We lit candles daily for eight days and sang "Ma'oz Tzur" every evening of the holiday. My father had sentimental memories of holidays in his childhood home and insisted on singing every verse of the song.

My mother and I did not know the words and preferred eating to singing. We often urged my father to finish or at least speed things up. Generally, we were unsuccessful.

There were few gifts in our household. This may have been because even before the war there was tremendous anti-Jewish tension in Hungary, and my parents considered it inappropriate to give gifts while thousands of Jewish men were being abused and starved in the Labor Service. However, they made an exception in 1942. I had begged for a new doll: I wanted one with limbs that could move and that could be dressed as fashionably as my mother and I were dressed. Much to my delight, my wish came true on the first night of Chanukah. My parents walked into my room, each holding one hand of a gorgeous doll. She was dressed in an embroidered Hungarian peasant dress, and she wore white shoes and socks. I instantly named her Zsuzsi, and we became inseparable. (Many years later, Zsuzsi would find a home at the US Holocaust Memorial Museum in Washington, DC.) My mother designed a beautiful outfit for Zsuzsi and I was able to help with the sewing. The coat and hat were made of off-white wool, recycled from a white sweater that had shrunk in the wash. Both the coat and hat were trimmed in orange. The project took several days. We worked late one winter evening to finish. As we heard nearby church bells chime seven times, signaling my bedtime, my face clouded over because I wanted to finish. Mother smiled and said we'd stay there together to complete the outfit for Zsuzsi. I was ecstatic.

Working on art projects with my mother was fun and always a treat. I was very proud to use her art materials. She had been trained in art and design at the Iparmüvészeti Iskola institute of applied arts in Budapest. She appreciated beautiful things: furniture, rugs, porcelain, silver, art, and nice clothes. Both of us had lovely, stylish wardrobes.

Anyuka also enjoyed leather tooling, and occasionally I helped her make leather flowers, which she sold to women as lapel decorations. When she did china painting, I was sometimes allowed to paint a flower or two.

There were beautiful tablecloths, china, silver, and crystal that were stored away in our home, though we rarely used them. For our daily meals we used a damask tablecloth with gold-rimmed porcelain dishes, but we rarely used the exceptionally beautiful things I so often heard about.

For one very special occasion, we used all the beautiful tableware. My mother's brother, Uncle Laszlo, whom we called Laci—born Imre Laszlo Havas in Honcto, Hungary, which became Gurahont, Romania, in 1908—was my mother's only sibling. He married Aunt Pircsi at the Dohány utca synagogue, the famous big synagogue in Budapest ("utca" is Hungarian for "street"). It was my first and possibly only time in the synagogue as a child, and I felt very uncomfortable there. It was cold and damp, and the rabbi was unfriendly. After the ceremony, attended only by the bride and groom, my parents, and me, we returned to our home for a festive wedding dinner. I don't recall what we ate, but I do remember being impressed with the beautifully appointed table.

Our apartment had no central heat. Every room but the bathroom had a fireplace or stove, but it was still always cold in the winter. There was one ritual that warmed me: Every evening, the maid brought a large washbasin to my room and placed it in front of the fireplace. She came back repeatedly with pitchers of hot water, pouring them into the basin until it was almost full. Then I climbed in, and my mother washed me from head to toe. I loved this nightly ritual, mostly because I had my mother's full attention.

My father's full attention took some time to win. Apuka's heart had been set on having a son. Having a daughter was such a disappointment that at first he barely acknowledged my existence, disappointing my mother. At some point, either he or I did something right because ultimately he became a very attentive father.

Apuka loved to ice-skate, and when I was about three, he bought me my first set of three-bladed training skates. Since my mother wasn't crazy about skating, it became my father's and my exclusive activity.

We skated outdoors almost daily in cold weather. At first I insisted on holding Apuka's hand, but with his encouragement I soon learned to skate independently. He bought me regular single-bladed skates the following year, and I was terrified to use them. We again began by holding hands, and then my father let go and skated backward in front of me. Much to my amazement, I quickly gained confidence on the new skates.

We usually skated during the dinner hour. The outdoor skating rink was located midway between our home and his office, and after skating, around 1:00, we walked home for dinner. On Sundays, when he had no office hours, he sometimes bought me hard candy on the way home. I was allowed one piece and was sworn to secrecy because my mother disapproved.

Once, when I was about four years old, I was being very disobedient. I don't recall what I was doing wrong, but my father's threats to throw away the candy did nothing to improve my behavior. As I continued to misbehave, he took the candy from my hands and threw the whole bag into a trash receptacle. I couldn't believe it. I cried all the way home, but I was much better behaved from then on.

Békés, my mother's hometown in southeast Hungary, was our annual summer destination. It was our respite from the oppressive heat of Budapest. Before the days of air conditioning, our fourth-floor apartment became intolerably hot during the summer months. Additionally, all household help went home to their family farms to help with the harvest. Food preparation and housekeeping were not a high priority in their absence, and my parents thought I'd be more comfortable with my grandparents in Békés. Békés was a town of about 20,000 residents. There were no tall buildings or traffic, and my grandparents' yard was shaded by mature walnut trees. Békés also provided freedom I lacked in Budapest. In Budapest, I went everywhere with an adult. In Békés, I was allowed time on my own.

Iren and Jakab Havas, my nagymama and nagyapa, had a roomy house with a shady yard. They lived within a few blocks of the Körös River, where we often swam. Unfortunately the river was dirty, and I rarely went in the water.

Békés meant fun. Apuka sometimes joined us for a few days, and Anyuka generally stayed for a couple of weeks. My mother was a different person in Békés. She smiled more and was more spontaneous and fun-loving than at home. Being the only Havas grandchild, I was a VIP, and I relished my importance.

One day Uncle Laci had promised to take me for a walk, and I waited outside on the bottom step of Grandmother's porch. I heard Uncle Laci's motorcycle before I saw him. Once in front of the house, he jumped off the motorbike and ran to me. When he picked me up, I squealed with delight as we waltzed from one end of the yard to the other.

We agreed to visit the bar and liquor store that was Nagyapa's business and the family's livelihood. Holding hands, we walked the two short blocks and went inside. In contrast to the heat and bright sun outdoors, the bar was cool and dark. Nagyapa was standing behind the counter, and his face lit up like the sun when he saw me. After giving me a big wet kiss on the cheek, he asked, "What flavor soda would you like today?" I requested raspberry: It was my favorite. Nagyapa provided a tall glass of raspberry soda, and I happily sat down to drink it.

Afterward, Uncle Laci and I continued our walk, stopping to admire the artesian well near the center of town. Hot and hungry, we soon went home for dinner. There was always a smile on Uncle Laci's face, a mischievous twinkle in his eye, and a plan for some wonderful activity taking shape in his head. He had time for me, no matter how busy he was. I once begged for a ride on his motorcycle but was told I'd have to wait until I was older.

My Békés grandparents loved my father. Whenever he visited, Nagymama was in the kitchen by 5:00 a.m. to bake breakfast sweets for him. On those mornings we awoke to the wonderful aroma of cinnamon-flavored sweet rolls. My father frequently quipped that going to Békés resulted in a five-kilo weight gain.

I was fascinated by the typewriter in front of a window in my grandparents' living room. Nagyapa placed some paper in the carriage and encouraged me to type. I diligently sat there and copied the words from a sign across the street. My grandparents were amazed and declared me a genius. For the rest of that summer, all visitors to the house were regaled with stories of my amazing feat. The attention did not embarrass me in the least; I loved it. Everything I did made my nagyapa smile. He fully enjoyed life, and an angry or negative word never seemed to leave his mouth.

During my 1942 summer visit to Békés, I contracted a severe case of measles. I was so ill that my mother was summoned from Budapest. My recovery was slow, and I grew bored. Uncle Laci's wife, Aunt Pircsi, was my mother's dear childhood friend and my favorite relative. She visited daily and usually asked if there was anything I needed. My typical answer was no. But one day when Pircsi asked, I replied, "Get me a watch." This was a gutsy request: Watches were scarce and expensive. My parents both had nice watches, and I wanted to copy them. Aunt Pircsi looked surprised and said, "I'll see what I can do." She didn't have much money. A few days later she came back carrying a small gift-wrapped package. "Here's a little present for you," she said as she handed it to me. I opened the box and found a small silver-colored watch with a perforated red leather band.

It was the most exciting gift I had ever received. I wore that watch every day in Hungary—and little did I know that I'd wear it in Bergen-Belsen, in Switzerland, and eventually in the United States. Even when my parents gave me a new watch as a high school graduation gift, the old watch found a home in the back of a drawer. Much to my dismay, it was gone when I looked for it years later.

Those early Békés summers were happy times. They were unregulated, cheerful vacations, escapes from the realities of daily life where the focus was on me.

CHAPTER 2

Digging Deeper

My paternal great-grandfather was Samuel Goldmann. He was a mashgiach: someone who supervises any kind of establishment that deals with kosher food—slaughterhouses, restaurants, grocers, butchers—as well as the utensils and other equipment used there to establish their adherence to laws of Kashrut, the laws concerning kosher Jewish food preparation. I have no idea what kind of a living that profession provided.

My paternal grandmother, Roza Feuerlicht, was born in Nagykereki, Hungary, in 1879. Nagymama Roza's lineage can be traced back to a rabbinic dynasty with a long line of notable rabbis and scholars. Roza was orphaned at an early age when her widowed mother, my great-grandmother Leah Planer Feuerlicht, died in 1889 at age 42. From then on, Roza was raised by an unknown aunt.

JUTKA

Mor Goldmann, my paternal grandfather, was born in 1874 in Fülek, Hungary (now Fil'akovo, Slovakia). When he came of age Mor enrolled in rabbinical school, but tuition was high and at some point, he ran out of money. He then transferred to teachers' college, which was more affordable, and became a certified teacher. His first job was in Egbell, Hungary (now Gbely, Slovakia). His next job was over 200 miles away, in Erdőbénye, Hungary. I have a copy of the letter of recommendation from his first job to his second, dated 1898. He taught there for a number of years.

It was in Erdőbénye that Mor met and married my grandmother Roza, around 1899. Being a certified teacher meant that he was a government employee. At that time, the Hungarian government strongly encouraged its employees to change their surnames to something that sounded Hungarian. Goldmann is a Germanic name, so Mor changed his name to "Gondos." This was probably about 1904, because my father was born a Goldmann in 1903 and then became a Gondos, which is my maiden name.

Mor and Roza's five children—Ilona (known as Ilonka), Zelma, my father Bela, Sandor (known as Sanyi), and Zoltan (known as Zoli)—were all born in Erdőbénye. Roza's sister, Sarolta, who was deaf, also lived with them. They were supported by my grandfather's very modest teacher's salary. My grandmother Roza made most of the family's clothes, including Mor's fine shirts. As a teacher, Mor became a summertime tutor for the children of a Czech nobleman who lived just across the border from them. Unfortunately, Mor had no passport or other documents to legally cross, so he regularly had to sneak across the Czech border.

As my father told me, Mor's two daughters—who my father said were very attractive—would go to the border with their father at night and engage the border guards, take their arms, and joke with them. While the guards were distracted, Mor would sneak across the border. My father and his brothers would use the same ruse to cross over to see their father. Then they'd arrange to do the same when they needed to cross back over the border to come home.

Then my grandfather was drafted into the army for World War I. His wages were likely minimal or nonexistent, and with five children and a sister to feed, my grandmother was desperate. She decided to seek advice from the Rebbe, an ultraconservative Chassidic rabbi in Bodrogkeresztúr, a small community about 10 miles from Erdőbénye.

My grandmother went to see the Rebbe on a Friday, presumably by horse-drawn carriage. She told him her story, and in response, he said, "Everything will be all right." That was great news, but he did not elaborate, and by this time it was nearly sunset. Observant Jews do not travel on the Sabbath. My grandmother had to spend the night at the Rebbe's home. She was astounded at the opulence: At dinner, they each got their own challah.

Late the next day, when she could travel again, my grandmother left for home. Lo and behold, the Rebbe was right: By the time she arrived, my grandpa had received word that his military duties were over and he was being sent home. Life resumed, and Mor got a better job, a principalship in Sátoraljaújhely, a town about 20 miles away. It came with a house, and they had a more comfortable life from that point on.

It was in Sátoraljaújhely that Mor developed empyema, a bacterial infection. They took him to Budapest, but doctors couldn't treat him. Grandpa Mor died there of empyema in 1931. He was 57 years old. I never met him.

In my father's family, he, Sandor, and Zoltan attended school and were encouraged to excel. The two girls, Ilonka, the eldest, and Zelma, the second-born child, attended school in the lower grades but later stayed home presumably to help their mother. Formal secondary school education seemed unlikely, possibly for financial reasons. My cousin Gordon Gondos believes Ilonka and Zelma benefitted from further instruction, as non-matriculated students. With neither financial resources nor a secondary school diploma, university education would have been an unrealistic goal.

In the summer of 1941, my parents told me we'd be taking the train to Mezőkövesd to visit my paternal grandmother, Roza, her sister Sarolta, Aunt Zelma, and Zelma's three sons. Mezőkövesd is about 75 miles northeast of Budapest, so our trip was planned as a one-day outing. Nagymama Roza often visited us in Budapest, but I had never been to Mezőkövesd and had not met Sarolta, Zelma, and the three cousins. I looked forward to getting to know them.

Mezőkövesd, a town of about 21,000, was small enough for us to explore on foot. After several hours of outdoor time and endless picture-taking, we entered the family home. From the very sunny outdoors we were ushered into a small, dark apartment. All family members were warm and hospitable, but I couldn't understand why all six of them lived in two rooms. Everything in the apartment seemed clean and orderly, but the congestion was depressing. The floors were bare, without any rugs. The few upholstered pieces were threadbare, no pictures adorned the walls, and the apartment lacked decoration. I was uncomfortable. No one had ever told me about poverty. When I sought an explanation, my mother signaled for me to be quiet.

Our visit ended in late afternoon, and we boarded the train home to Budapest. This time my mother tried to explain why Zelma was so poor. The situation was complicated, as most such things are. Over a period of many years, my parents shared several brutal facts.

As noted earlier, Sarolta, my grandmother's sister, was deaf. She had attended a residential school for the deaf, but there were no available jobs when she finished school. Sarolta's marriage prospects were dim because of her auditory challenges and lack of a dowry. She and my grandmother had several brothers, but they all declined to contribute to her support. My father, a struggling young roentgenologist (the original term for radiologist), asked his own uncles for help. He, too, received negative responses. My grandfather Mor was supporting five children on a teacher's salary and questioned his ability to provide for an additional household member. Out of other options, my grandparents invited Sarolta to join their household. My father explained that Sarolta, fit and able physically and mentally, was a great help to the Gondos family. Later, when the war was underway, Sarolta and my grandmother Roza both were deported to Auschwitz and presumably were sent to the gas chambers soon after their arrival there.

Zelma also had a sad story. Like her Aunt Sarolta, Zelma had neither a dowry nor a profession. She married Lajos Adler, who was drafted into the Labor Service very early in World War II and died in Ukraine. Zelma and Lajos had no savings, and the family had no source of income after Lajos left. My grandmother, then living comfortably as a widow on Mor's teachers' pension, had planned to move to Budapest. Recognizing Zelma's need, Roza moved instead—with her sister Sarolta—to Mezőkövesd, where she shared a home with Zelma and her boys. A widow's pension, comfortable for one, was now barely supporting six people. This explained the impoverished environment we encountered in Mezőkövesd.

Many years later, on one of our walks in Rock Creek Park near Washington, DC, my father told me Zelma had always wanted a teaching career, and he had planned to send her to teachers' college after the war. Unfortunately, that never happened because she did not survive the Holocaust.

When people reached the concentration camps, they were separated first by gender: One line for men and one for women. Then they were separated again into those who could work and those who could not.

We have found records of my maternal grandfather's death in Auschwitz and of Zelma's as well, but nothing on the fates of Iren, Roza, Sarolta, and the boys. (The Nazis kept impeccable records, but only about those who worked. Roza and Sarolta were too old and the three boys too young to work. Because there were no records of them, almost certainly my maternal grandmother, my paternal grandmother, her sister Sarolta, and my three cousins all went directly from the boxcars to the Auschwitz gas chambers.)

On my mother's side, my maternal grandfather was born Jakab Hochwald in Körösbökény, Hungary, in 1882. He was one of quite a few children. Because of the pressure to adopt a more Hungarian name, Jakab changed his surname from Hochwald to Havas in 1904, as did his brother Adolf, who later changed his first name to Abraham.

Jakab married my grandmother, Iren Bleuer, in 1906. Iren was born in Békés in 1886. Early in their marriage, Jakab and his brother ran a lumber business in Honcto, Hungary, that they apparently took over from their father.

My mother, Anna Ilona (nicknamed Ilus) Havas, was born in Honcto on June 22, 1910. After World War I, through the Treaty of Trianon that was prepared at the Paris Peace Conference of 1919 in Versailles and signed there on June 4, 1920, Hungary lost nearly two-thirds of its territory. It was through that treaty that Honcto, Hungary, became Gurahont, Romania. When that happened my grandfather left his hometown and his business and moved to Békés, Hungary, my grandmother's hometown. They left everything behind because Jakab Havas considered himself to be a Hungarian, not a Romanian.

My mother and father were married in Békés on August 14, 1934. Jakab's mother, Terez, attended the wedding, as did brothers Salamon and Emil, who also served as witnesses. Uncle Moritz Bleuer, owner of a successful export/import business, had assumed responsibility for making all of his newly married nieces and nephews economically self-sufficient. In my parents' case, he fully equipped my father's radiology office, enabling him to immediately start a private radiology practice.

Previously my father had studied under students who had been taught directly by Wilhelm Conrad Roentgen, the father of radiology. In 1895 at the University of Würzburg, in Germany, Roentgen was conducting experiments using electron beams from a cathode-ray tube and glass when he noticed something that could pass through flesh and record images on photographic plates. A famous early one is of his wife's hand with only her bones and her wedding ring showing. He called them "X-rays," not knowing what it was he had discovered. In 1901, Roentgen was awarded the very first Nobel Prize in physics for his discovery. At some point, my father attended a lecture in Vienna where Roentgen himself was a speaker.

Grandfather Jakab Havas went into the liquor business in Békés and was successful. He opened a small distillery, a liquor bottling plant, a wholesale liquor establishment, and neighborhood bar downtown, no more than two blocks from the Havas home.

I often visited him and always received a syrupy sweet drink, a "Havas Jakab" concoction. I think Nagymama disapproved of these sweet drinks. Being the family disciplinarian, she often told my grandfather that the treats would spoil my appetite for supper or dinner.

Nagyapa was always happy, definitely not a disciplinarian. I don't think he ever argued with my grandmother, but I do recall that he continued to treat me to sweet beverages despite her admonitions. He was a very sweet man and an attentive grandfather. One day he took me to an ice cream shop owned by a good friend on the far side of the town's artesian well. He bought me my first ice cream cone there. The ice cream was orange flavored and delicious. I excitedly waved the cone around, but my small hands were unable to keep it balanced. The ice cream fell off the cone and hit the floor. I cried and cried. The kind shop owner offered to replace it for me, but I was inconsolable, and I refused his offer. Nagyapa took my hand and said he'd buy me another cone the following summer. Sadly, he was never able to fulfill his promise. He was bedridden with heart disease the following year and was subsequently deported to Auschwitz and murdered in the gas chambers there, June 30, 1944.

CHAPTER 3

A Bitter Understanding

Békés was the site of my earliest exposure to antisemitism. Although our home in Budapest was not in a Jewish neighborhood, my parents' social lives were centered around Jewish contacts and family. My friends, too, were Jewish. The antisemitism that had always existed in Hungary intensified in the early 1940s, but my exposure had been limited. In Békés, with a Jewish population of a few hundred, my grandparents had endured antisemitic acts for decades. Although Jews and Christians mixed socially, Jews often were subjected to virulent antisemitic acts. Taking advantage of Jews had become a national pastime.

My first exposure to this was the loss of Nagyapa's thriving business. In 1938, the Hungarian Parliament enacted its Jewish laws which were actually anti-Jewish laws. It was patterned after Germany's Nuremberg Laws of 1935. The Hungarian Jewish laws were amended and augmented multiple times and placed severe restrictions on the lives of the Jewish population. These restrictions covered most facets of everyday existence: political rights, human rights, economic rights, legal rights. As a result of that law's restrictions on Jewish economic activity, Jakab Havas no longer was allowed to own his business. In about 1942, he was forced to sell his bar/liquor store and brewery/bottling plant for a token sum to his longtime manager and good friend, Feher Margit. In the unwritten part of their agreement, Margit promised Jakab a managerial position, including a comfortable salary.

But without explanation, Nagyapa was demoted shortly after the ownership transfer and was soon fired by his former friend. My grandparents had invested most of their assets in the business and were left with no means of livelihood and limited liquid assets.

These issues were freely discussed in my presence in Békés. Although no one gave me a detailed explanation, I understood some things that were happening, but not why. Even today, although I realize and appreciate that Hungarians alive now played no actual part in the heinous treatment of the Jews—of us—during World War II, I continue to be uncomfortable with Hungarians and continue to harbor resentment toward Hungary and Hungarians in general.

My second exposure to antisemitism, though indirect, also occurred in Békés. The Jewish Laws of the late 1930s limited the amount of money and gold Jews lawfully could possess. They were required to "lend" all valuable holdings to the government. Nagyapa and Laci had no faith in the government, certain they'd never get their money and valuables back. They purchased gold coins and jewelry and buried them in a circle around the defunct well in their backyard. I didn't see them do it, but it was discussed in my presence. Interestingly, the house was seized for back taxes after World War II and later razed. No gold was found anywhere on its premises. During a visit to Békés with my children and grandchildren Diane, Dan, Tom, Jonathan, and Max, we carefully looked for the well, hoping to find the hidden treasure buried nearby. Unfortunately, we found neither the well nor the treasure.

My third exposure to antisemitic activity involved Uncle Laci. He was one of the first in the family to be conscripted into the Hungarian Labor Service. During World War II, Jews were considered unworthy to serve in the army. Instead, able-bodied Jewish men were conscripted into the Labor Service. They were untrained, ill-equipped, and not transported as regular soldiers were. More often, they walked. Their work for the Hungarian Army was usually menial, such as ditch-digging, latrine-building, road construction. It was often dangerous, as when sweeping for mines by being made to walk through the minefields. They provided free labor to the Hungarian Army, and their absence from home deprived their families of income, devastating the Jewish economy.

One evening during my summer visit in 1941, Laci kissed me goodnight as I went to bed; he was gone when I awoke the following morning. We never saw him again.

At first there were letters from him, often requesting packages. Jakab and Iren sent him whatever he needed. During that first summer, I helped assemble a package for Laci. There was warm clothing, including a jacket, warm slacks, a sweater, socks, and a scarf. My grandmother sewed gold coins and gold jewelry into the linings. Cigarettes were also included in the package. Iren and Jakab hoped the gold and cigarettes would have barter value should Laci try to gain his freedom.

Lastly, they included a variety of nonperishable food items, including hard candy. There was a wartime shortage of sugar, and I had not eaten candy for a long time. I begged for a piece. I cried. My request was denied because, as Nagymama explained, Laci needed the candy more than I did.

My father was conscripted twice into the Labor Service. His first posting was in Székesfehérvár. He was released after serving a few months, but he was again conscripted; this time he was sent to Szentkirályszabadja, about 70 miles southwest of Budapest. Szentkirályszabadja was a temporary stop for his battalion. I assume my parents corresponded, but I heard nothing from or about my father for months. To my great surprise and pleasure, my mother announced one day that she and I would travel by train to visit my father in Szentkirályszabadja. The train trip took a few hours, and upon arrival we were met by a skinny, unkempt man wearing dirty, ill-fitting clothes. I realized only when he ran to hug my mother that the man was my father. After a brief exchange of pleasantries, we sat down on a nearby bench. Realizing we were in my father's company, I was ecstatic and didn't want to leave his side. My mother passed some papers to Bela. He placed them in his pocket, and then it was time to board our train and return home to Budapest.

The train trip to Szentkirályszabadja was significant. At the beginning of the war, Regent Miklós Horthy (who led the Kingdom of Hungary from 1920 until the Nazi occupation in March 1944) appointed physicians to serve in an antiaircraft civil defense emergency hospital, the "rock hospital," secluded inside a Buda cave. My father had received a letter of appointment. After a few weeks at his second Labor Service posting, my father learned that his entire battalion was to be sent east from Szentkirályszabadja. Fearing he would not return home alive, my father seized the opportunity provided by the letter of appointment to the civil defense emergency hospital. My mother brought the document to Szentkirályszabadja, and my father showed it to the commanding officer. The officer was impressed and sent Bela home to Pest. My father's Labor Service unit was sent east, and no one in that group was heard from again.

My fourth and fifth exposures to antisemitism occurred the following summer. The Békés churches overtly spewed antisemitic venom during services, resulting in public displays of hate and embarrassment. At about the same time, the schools began to exclude Jewish students.

Nagymama and I sat in the shade of the walnut tree in the backyard one very hot Sunday. Her goal was to teach me origami, a skill at which she excelled. I was fascinated by the things she crafted out of paper, but I was not at all interested in reproducing the boxes and airplanes she made. I preferred running around and picking up falling walnuts, many of which hit us on the head. As I collected these walnuts, I heard a ruckus on the street and saw, through the slats in the iron fence, a wagon with elaborately dressed, very loud young people approaching our house. Without explanation, grandma whisked me inside and instructed me not to leave the house for the rest of the day.

Nagymama refused to discuss what was happening. My mother arrived in Békés a few days later, and I asked her about the preceding Sunday's events. She explained that Békés was heavily populated by uneducated farmers. Church on Sunday mornings, which included venomous anti-Jewish sermons, was their common activity. Incited by the vitriol they had heard, many local residents headed straight for the taverns immediately after church, probably including my grandfather's. Under the influence of alcohol, they entertained themselves by riding around town in their wagons, harassing all the Jews they encountered.

A second incident occurred during the same visit. Grandma and I were sitting under the same walnut tree. This time she was trying to teach me how to embroider. My enthusiasm for embroidery resembled my reaction to origami. As in the past, I spent the bulk of my time running around picking up walnuts. Grandmother exercised restraint and did not overtly show displeasure at my lack of interest. I do believe, though, that she was disappointed.

At one point we both looked through the fence and saw my cousin Eva approaching the house. Eva was the daughter of Nagymama's brother, Emil, and their family lived on the first floor of the house where my grandparents lived. Eva, about 11 or 12 at the time, was bent over with the weight of an overloaded book bag, and she was sobbing. Alarmed, Nagymama and I ran to help, hoping we could. In response to Nagymama's questions, Eva replied, "All the Jewish students were expelled from school today." I was sad and puzzled, but again, no explanation was forthcoming. Eva was later deported and died at the Stutthof concentration camp, according to our cousin, Gabor Hirsch.

Late in 1942, in Budapest, it was time to find a school for me to attend the following September. My parents chose a Jewish day school not far from home. It was a fine institution; it worked out well, and I liked everything about the school. However, initially I wondered why other schools had not been considered. Much later, my parents explained that Jewish students were no longer allowed to enroll in secular schools.

First grade began in September 1943. My school was part of the Jewish Boys' Orphanage. The orphans, all boys, wore shabby dark uniforms. There was very little interaction between the orphans and the day school students, because we were discouraged from socializing with them. Our teacher there was Margit néni (not to be confused with nanny Margit in Budapest, nor my nagyapa's treacherous business partner Margit in Békés). This Margit, our teacher, was very formal and taught primarily by lecture, with no input from the students. She was often distraught, worried about the fate of her husband, who had been conscripted into the Labor Service.

The start of the heavy bombing of Budapest followed the start of school, and we missed many days of classes. I don't recall attending school at all after winter break of 1943.

By 1943 we had very limited household help, and our home took on a semineglected look. There was a food shortage, and we no longer ate the good meals to which we were accustomed. My mother, an inexperienced cook, prepared the best meals she could. We had no meat and generally ate pasta, dumplings, and eggs. Nearby farms supplied enough fruits and vegetables, and we managed to get enough to eat. In the absence of a better cook and presumably better ingredients, there were no home-baked desserts.

Our days were no longer pre-planned, because of frequent air raids, and we spent many nights in the air raid shelter at Rottenbiller utca 35. A large section of the basement had been cleared for this purpose, and most of the building's residents gathered there when the sirens sounded. Generally, we went to bed fully dressed with a small carry-on bag nearby, ready for the sirens. I loved going to the shelter. Once there, I was able to play with my cousin, Nomi, and the other kids in the building. We all brought our favorite toys, ate snacks, and got to stay up late and play. What could be better?

I was convinced our building would never be bombed. After all, my Uncle Zoltan, "Zoli," lived in the United States, and he would tell the pilots not to bomb our apartment house. Surprisingly, the building suffered no apparent bomb damage during the war.

Heavy bombing continued during the winter of 1943–1944. To deter bombers, the government issued a mandate requiring all windows to be fully covered with a dark shade, preventing the escape of visible light outdoors in the evenings. Slipups, though rare, occurred from time to time. Any infraction of this law was punishable, much more so if the guilty party was Jewish. Incarceration and devastatingly large fines were imposed on Jews for the smallest infractions.

On a particularly cold winter day, exhausted from multiple trips to the bomb shelter, a kindly non-Jewish neighbor (there were very few of those) came to inform my mother that light was streaming out from our window and a policeman was writing a report to the authorities. My mother immediately went into action. From her wallet, she pulled a roll of pengos, the Hungarian currency at the time, and headed downstairs, hoping to catch the policeman before he left. He was just finishing his report as my mother approached. With a smile and profuse apologies, coupled with promises to be more careful in the future, she handed him the roll of bills. The officer smiled, accepted the money, and tore up the report.

We had very little money by this time, and using it as a bribe, though effective, deprived us of the necessities of life—food in particular. However, the danger of incarceration and a larger fine had made this the chosen course of action.

My father, as a busy radiologist, had always made time to ice-skate with me. By late 1943 he had plenty of time. Antisemitism was so prevalent that non-Jewish patients refused to consult Jewish physicians. There was demand for medical care in the Jewish community, but no available compensation. The Jewish economy had deteriorated dramatically, and Jews were unable to pay for medical services. As a result, our family income dwindled to near nothing, but my father continued to maintain his practice where he saw a patient only every now and then.

The community maintained a medical facility for indigent Jews, Budapesti Orthodox Izraelita Hiitkozseg Nyilvanos Rendelo Intezete Szegeny Betegek Reszere (Budapest Orthodox Israelite Community Official Facility for the Indigent Sick), located on Kertész utca. For many years my father worked there daily as a volunteer radiologist. He began to see patients on Kertész utca around 7:30 a.m. We ate a rushed, very early breakfast together. Occasionally, my father skipped breakfast altogether in order to get to Kertész utca on time. I was resentful that my father left us so early in the morning. However, he instilled in me the obligation for Jewish communal service at a very early age. Bela headed for his own office on Andrasi at about 9:30.

While Bela was in the Labor Service, my mother worked very hard to provide for us. She ran a profitable rug business with my maternal grandmother, Iren, after my grandfather Jakab's businesses were confiscated.

The rug business was a golden opportunity because imported Oriental rugs were unavailable, but people still needed to cover their floors. Mother designed the rugs, which were manufactured in Békés. Békés had a sizable labor force, and many farm laborers were available after the harvest. Weaving supplies were relatively inexpensive. Nagymama purchased the raw materials and oversaw the weaving of colorful rugs in a house my grandparents owned. The finished rugs were shipped to Budapest, where my mother sold them.

Mother needed someone to take care of me while she ran her

part of the rug business. By this time, non-Jewish women were unwilling to work in Jewish homes, and we had a succession of household helpers as a result. Their main job was to watch me in my mother's absence. Some were bad, and some were even worse. We were fortunate when Goldberg Klari came our way.

Klari was a small red-haired woman with a heavy German accent. She told me very little about her background, but I knew she was a musician, and she taught me piano and singing. Her voice, in my opinion, was not as operatic as she seemed to think, though it was pleasant. Klari came to our home almost daily. When there were no air raids and when the weather was nice, we went for walks in the neighborhood. She and I bonded and really enjoyed one another's company. Occasionally, I asked her about her family. Did she have a husband and children, siblings, parents? Her responses were vague.

At the end of a very pleasant outing several months after she had joined us, Klari asked my mother to sit down with her. They sent me to my room while they talked. Neither of them shared the subject of their conversation with me, but when they were finished, Klari kissed me goodbye and left. I never saw her again.

After the war, my mother explained the situation. During that last conversation, Klari said to my mother, "Ilus, these are dangerous times. People often come into your lives for a short time and then you never see them again. It is safer for everyone if you do not know who they are, where they came from, and where they are going. And you should never ask any questions." We never learned Klari's real name. My mother inferred that

Klari was in Hungary illegally and that she was probably going into hiding. The Hungarian border remained unofficially open after the Nazi atrocities began, and many Jews, fleeing Nazi persecution elsewhere, found temporary refuge in Hungary.

Once Klari no longer came to be with me, my mother was again faced with the challenge of running the rug business and taking care of a young child. Gitta, who was Jewish, was our next helper. She came to us by word of mouth with acceptable, but not glowing, recommendations. Gitta was hired as household help and was accommodated in the maid's room. She was pleasant and friendly, and I liked her.

In spite of a food shortage in Budapest, my parents had a well-stocked pantry. Its contents came primarily from Békés, where food was more available. My mother began to notice a dwindling of our food supplies. She thought Gitta might be stealing food, but she wasn't sure. I overheard this discussion as she related the problem to Aunt Rozsi over the telephone. Mother never confirmed her suspicion about the missing food.

One evening, after I had gone to bed, I heard strong and loud language at the other end of our apartment. Being unaccustomed to raised voices, I was frightened and ran to see what was happening. My mother was yelling at Gitta, telling her to leave our home right away. Gitta did as she was told. I was sent back to bed and received no explanation. Gitta was gone when I got up the next morning. Years later, my mother told me she had found Gitta in bed with a strange man in our maid's room, necessitating her immediate dismissal.

After the rug business had successfully operated for a year

or more, two uniformed gendarmes unexpectedly arrested Nagymama in her Békés home. Falsely charged with operating a business without a license, she was dragged in handcuffs through the town square and was taken by train to a jail in Budapest.

Nagymama was a small, unassuming woman who never threatened anyone. All family members knew they could count on her to do what had to be done, at home and in the business. She was responsible for the financial aspects of the family business, and she oversaw a very well-run household. My grandmother was kind and attentive, but unlike Nagyapa, she was reserved and undemonstrative. Nagymama was overshadowed by Nagyapa's cheerfulness and affable personality.

Desperate about Nagymama's arrest, Nagyapa called my mother. With confidence she did not have, my mother assured him she'd take care of the problem.

Anyuka decided on a bold and dangerous plan. Dressed in her finest and carrying a large roll of currency in her coat pocket, she approached the prison. Without an appointment, she charmed her way to the superintendent's office. Once there, she told him her story, indicating her certainty that he would not want to hold an innocent elderly lady in his prison. (Nagymama was in her mid-fifties at the time.) As she shook his hand before leaving, Ilus passed the roll of bills to the superintendent. Trembling in fear, she hurried home. While the superintendent certainly could have ordered her arrest, imprisonment, or deportation to a concentration camp, within a few hours Nagymama was on a train bound for Békés. My mother had successfully bribed a government official.

Her second attempt did not go so well. Aunt Pircsi owned a dressmaking business in Békés. During wartime, when everything was scarce, she had accumulated a large inventory of fabrics. Not long before the Nazi occupation, local gendarmes unjustifiably arrested her. She was charged with illegal accumulation of inventory and sent to a Budapest prison.

Hoping to duplicate the efforts she had used for her mother's release, my mother was confident she could bribe officials to get Pircsi out of jail as well. Unfortunately, she was unable to get inside the jail at all. Aunt Pircsi languished in the Budapest prison and ultimately was sent to Auschwitz. She survived the death camp, but died of tuberculosis in Sweden just weeks after being liberated. The Swedes buried her and several other concentration camp survivors in Norrköping. Unlike the rest of our family murdered in the Holocaust, Aunt Pircsi has a headstone, a grave marker provided by the Swedes.

As World War II raged on, intense bombing of Budapest was relentless, and the effects of antisemitism intensified daily. Békés, home of my maternal grandparents, was no paradise, but my parents believed it might provide a safer and more normal environment for me.

Anyuka wrote to Nagyapa and Nagymama seeking their opinion about sending me to Békés, away from the threats of daily bombings. My very wise grandmother's response surprised them. She pointed out that I would always be welcome in their home at any time and for any length of time, and she emphasized how much they enjoyed my company and how very much they loved me. But in such uncertain and dangerous times, she and Nagyapa strongly felt that my place was with my parents.

Their wisdom saved my life. Grandma and Grandpa were deported from Békés to Auschwitz in late June 1944. We believe that they both died in the gas chambers there and their bodies were burned in the crematoria.

CHAPTER 4

The Nazis Arrive

Saturday, March 18, 1944, began as an uneventful day. There had been no air raids that morning, and I stood by the window of my room surveying the scene below. Ours was a corner apartment building, across the street from a multistoried German school. Until that point, it had served as an educational institution for German children in Budapest. The students wore uniforms smaller than, but similar to, those of the Nazi SS. My Jewish friends and I made fun of these kids in their stiff uniforms and the formal, similarly stiff manner in which they comported themselves. The German students marched around the school grounds many times on a typical day.

That Saturday morning, I was spellbound as I observed adult marchers, not the children we usually saw. Knowing this was unusual, I ran to tell my mother. She very calmly came to my window, looked at the uniformed students for a few minutes, then went back to whatever she had been doing. I repeatedly asked, "What's this all about? Why the adults?" I received no response to my questions. I assumed my mother did not consider the events across the street worthy of more than a momentary glance.

Later that afternoon, an unexpected visitor rang our doorbell. We feared unknown persons at our door, particularly since my nagymama's unjustified arrest. With trepidation, my father and mother answered the door. A man in civilian clothes introduced himself and indicated that someone we knew, though I have no idea who it was, had sent him to pass on some very important information. My parents invited him to join us and served refreshments. I was not sent to my room, as usual. This unexpected visitor informed us of a planned Nazi occupation the following day. He left immediately after sharing this news.

My parents were alarmed and spent most of the night discussing their very limited options. It was too late to obtain false papers to disappear, and fleeing the country seemed impossible because borders were officially closed. I assume they notified family and friends, but ultimately they took no action. Even I, a six-year-old, was mortified by the visitor's news, startling information that corroborated my concerns earlier in the day. The Nazis occupied Hungary the following day. By noon, their presence was common knowledge.

Although there was little to do at the office, my father continued to go to work as he always had. One morning, just a few days after the Nazi occupation, he was home about 10:00 a.m.

THE NAZIS ARRIVE

In response to my mother's questions, he related the following: He had arrived at his office at the usual time and was greeted by two well-dressed, very polite Gestapo men. They complimented him on his office and state-of-the-art equipment. The Germans, they went on to say, were honoring my father by planning to use his office as the radiology facility for Budapest-based German officers. They allowed my father 20 minutes to vacate the premises, permitting him to take anything that would fit in his pockets. He pleaded to take the medical records of some very ill patients who were undergoing radiation therapy with the goal of transferring them to someone else's care. The request was denied. After pocketing a few small items from his desk, Father left the office. For the rest of his life, he felt guilty about those records, feeling the loss was akin to abandoning his patients.

This episode marked the end of his practice of radiology in Hungary and of course deprived him of the small income he had still been able to generate. As far as I know, my father never returned to his office.

The Nazi occupation and persecution of the Jews brought out the worst in some people, yet the best in a very few others. We had limited contact with our Christian neighbors on Rottenbiller utca. We knew a few by name, others only by sight. There was a nice Christian family near us on the fourth floor. They were closer to the elevator than we were, and we often passed their apartment. We usually greeted one another, but I did not know their names. One evening, not long after the Nazi occupation, the doorbell rang. By that time, visitors to our home were scarce, and the ringing of the doorbell often meant trouble. Anxiously, my parents answered the door and were pleasantly surprised to find the man from down the hall. He had never been to our home before. The man came in and we sat down to talk. He explained that his conscience had driven him to us. Fearing he could do nothing for Pest's Jews, he thought he could save one: me. He invited me to join his family, where he would treat me as one of his own children. I could safely live with them as long as necessary, he explained. After the war, I would return to my parents. He asked for no financial compensation.

The gentleman was kind, and his offer was unbelievably thoughtful. He would have faced dire consequences had the Nazis found him in our home. This was my first time facing a difficult family decision. I don't know whether or not my parents had a change of heart, or circumstances prevented them from sending me to my room, as was their custom.

Without being asked, with tears in my eyes, I blurted out, "I don't want to go. I want to stay with you." The neighbor and my parents were stunned. My parents looked at each other, and the communication with their eyes reflected a decision. They profoundly thanked the neighbor for his very generous and selfless offer but explained that they felt it best for the family to stay together. I never knew or learned the name of this kindly gentleman and have no idea what became of him and his family.

Later that spring we received a postcard from my father's sister, Zelma, who had lived about 75 miles northeast of Budapest. This was our first communication from family since the Nazi occupation. The handwriting was familiar, but the postmark

THE NAZIS ARRIVE

was foreign. In very stilted language, Zelma indicated she was working in a remote community, she was healthy, and she had enough to eat. My parents were puzzled and seemed not to understand the realities behind Zelma's communication. They learned only after the war that the Nazis, hoping to allay fear, often forced deportees to write to their families with positive news. After the war's end, we learned through the Red Cross that Zelma was deported to Auschwitz on August 2, 1944. She was transferred to Buchenwald on September 19 and sent back to Auschwitz on October 27, where she was murdered.

As part of the Nazi-enforced reign of terror, anti-Jewish regulations followed one after another in rapid succession, the first of which was the wearing of a yellow star, mandatory for all Jews whenever they left their homes. Its purpose was easy identification and possibly added humiliation. For me, the yellow star seemed like an attractive decoration: I had a royal blue spring coat, and I thought the yellow star enhanced its appearance. It was very striking on the heavily textured wool of my coat.

Our time away from home was restricted to two hours in the afternoon, making grocery shopping very difficult, if not impossible. Grocers' shelves were bare by the time Jews were permitted to shop. There was almost nothing left to buy. Therefore the hunger, which had plagued us for months, was now exacerbated. Meat was scarce, and whatever became available was not kosher. Out of perceived necessity, my father became a vegetarian. My mother and I ate whatever we found in the markets, which was generally very little.

The streets themselves were not forbidden to Jews, but use of public transportation was not allowed, and all privately owned cars and bicycles had been confiscated. We were not permitted to leave the city, but where could we go on foot?

Jews were not allowed to congregate anywhere—not in theaters, synagogues, museums, or parks. JEWS NOT ALLOWED signs were seen even on the benches that lined the streets.

My mother was very cautious, and we left our home only when absolutely necessary. We'd heard of Nazis apprehending Jews on the streets, marching them to the Danube and shooting them into the river. (In fact, there is now a monument to those Jews who suffered that particular fate: a sculpture of empty shoes.) My parents were aware of deportations, but they seemed not to know where the trains were headed and what happened when they arrived at their destinations. Perhaps they could identify Oświęcim, Poland, geographically. However, Auschwitz (the German name for Oświęcim) and the related atrocities were unknown to them.

The Nazis had taken our telephone. Mail and newspapers were heavily censored. Travel was impossible. The result was that the Jews of Budapest were isolated and uninformed.

Our lives were punctuated by fear and uncertainty. We had no idea what was happening to our families in the provinces, and we didn't know what would happen to us. The bombing of the city continued, but we were no longer permitted the safety of the bomb shelter. We had to congregate in the glass-walled entrance lobby of the apartment building. We didn't know who or what would get us first, the Nazis or the bombs. In addition to food shortages, we would soon run out of money.

THE NAZIS ARRIVE

My parents had tried to shield me from Nazi brutality in Budapest. They never explained what was happening. They must have believed the less I knew, the better off I would be. If apprehended, there would be nothing to disclose, and in the meantime, perhaps, I could lead a more normal life. I think they may have underestimated my powers of observation and my sensitivities.

I saw them tremble in fear whenever there was a knock on the door. Would there be terrible news about my grandparents? Or about my Uncle Laci, in the Labor Service?

I observed the trepidation with which they left home to buy what food they could. Would they come home from such outings, or would they be apprehended by the Nazis, jailed, deported, or shot?

"Be as inconspicuous as possible," my mother always said. This meant being quiet, casting my eyes downward, and never, never making eye contact with the Nazis. I was instructed to act like a mouse, not a human being.

Being an only child in the constant company of adults, I perceived much, but not all. I realized how awful things were, but not their implications. By that time, at age seven, I had learned to keep my mouth shut, my ears open, and my eyes cast downward.

While we were in Budapest, there was no ghetto as such. The Nazis designated about 2,000 apartment buildings as "Yellow Star Houses," compulsory Jewish residences. All of about 220,000 Jews in the city were ordered to move into one of them. Our building, which was close to the Jewish quarter, became a Star House. The spacious apartment that previously housed my parents and me and a maid now became home to many of our extended family.

Distant relatives, Pista bácsi and Rezi néni, moved into my room. I don't know their full names. My furniture was stacked in the entry hall, and I moved in with my parents. Although I had met Pista and Rezi, I did not know them well and at first was uneasy to have them in our home.

However, Pista and Rezi had a breakfront with glass doors, and there was a full candy dish on one of the shelves. They offered me candy when I had occasion to go to their room. One day when they were gone, I helped myself to a piece of fruit-flavored candy. It was delicious. Sugar was unavailable during the war years, and this forbidden treat tasted special. I enjoyed it so much that I repeatedly took candy when Rezi and Pista were gone, until one day I realized that there were only mint-flavored candies left, which I disliked. I'm sure Rezi and Pista had a good idea of what happened to the candy, but, to their credit, they never said a word.

My mother's aunt and uncle, Rozsi néni and Erno bácsi (Nagymama's brother, Erno) occupied another room. Rozsi and Erno had long been part of our lives, and I felt comfortable in their presence. Yet I didn't understand why all these relatives had to be in our home. It was overcrowded. The maid's room initially was used for storage, but later it too became an inhabited bedroom.

At first, we had communal meals at the large kitchen table. The friendly relationships must have become strained after a few days, and soon we ate alone in small family units.

Fear and helplessness continued as Nazi truculence intensified. Hungarians, Jews, and Christians alike were aware that

THE NAZIS ARRIVE

Hitler was losing the war. "Can we hang on long enough and manage until the war's end?" was the lingering question. My parents had serious doubts.

The Nazis had forbidden Jews to gather anywhere except the grounds of Jewish communal headquarters on Síp utca. The facility was closely monitored. Allegedly, the Gestapo had full information about those who attended, how long they stayed, even what they discussed.

My father, at the risk of being apprehended, walked there daily. It was about a 30-minute walk. Father, increasingly fearful of our fate in Budapest, was convinced he could gain useful information from others at the Síp utca facility. Though my mother feared for his safety and tried to discourage these outings, my father continued to go there. My parents, who rarely fought, exchanged harsh words before these daily trips.

My mother nervously paced the floor while my father was gone and sighed in relief each time he returned home, often with stories about people he knew. Some had been deported, others were jailed, and several of their friends simply had disappeared. They concluded they needed to take action to survive but had no idea what to do.

CHAPTER 5

A Glimmer of Hope

My father was introduced to Zionism while a student in secondary school. He had been visiting a non-Jewish friend whose aunt said, "Bela, you're such a nice boy. What a pity you're Jewish." This remark was both upsetting and incomprehensible, and he began to wonder how he, and all Jews, could live meaningful Jewish lives in peace without antisemitism. A Zionist periodical, *Új Kelet* (New Mid East), convinced my father that making aliyah (the term generally used for going to Palestine, literally "going up," as in "going up to Palestine, now Israel") was the only answer for Jews. At the university, he joined Maccabea, the student Zionist organization. Its members, all committed Zionists, became his lifelong friends.

Smiles and excitement illuminated my father's face as he arrived back home from Síp utca one afternoon in May of

1944. He had learned about a rescue train being organized by his fellow Zionists.

The rescue train, known as the Kasztner Train, resulted from negotiations between the Budapest Zionist leadership and the Nazis in Hungary. Adolph Eichmann, architect of Nazi deportations in Hungary, proposed "Blood for Goods," a deal to gain funds for the Nazis in return for Jewish lives. Eichmann's price was $1,000 a head, plus trucks and other goods, including a sizeable down payment. The balance of the ransom was due when the group reached the safety of a neutral country, Spain or Portugal. Eichmann negotiated with Rezso Kasztner, a Zionist leader and a journalist and lawyer by profession. Kasztner had enviable interpersonal communication skills.[1]

Doubtful about being able to deliver trucks, Kasztner agreed to Eichmann's demands. He embarked on a campaign to raise the necessary funds, but securing funding was difficult. Most Jews had turned over all of their money and valuables, although there were some who still had hidden assets. Seeking additional financial backing, Kasztner traveled to Switzerland to meet with the American Joint Distribution Committee, the Jewish Agency for Palestine (established in 1929 as the operative branch of the World Zionist Organization), and the War Refugee Board. Eichmann and Kasztner continued their contentious negotiations that ultimately transported 1,684[2] Jews to Bergen-Belsen and then to Switzerland.[3]

---

1   Ladislaus Löb, *Rezso Kasztner* (London: Random House, 2009).
2   Anna Porter, *Kasztner's Train* (Vancouver: Douglas & McIntyre Ltd, 2007).
3   Randolph L. Braham, *The Politics of Genocide* (New York: Columbia University Press, 1981), 955.

The Hungarian Zionist leadership was also faced with the challenge of compiling a list of passengers. The leadership allegedly tried to assemble a representative group. Applicants represented a broad swath of Hungarian Jewry, some from the provinces and others from Budapest, Zionists and non-Zionists, rich and poor, educated and uneducated. Some were just children. Many pleaded for the few available places on the train.[4]

My father applied for spaces on the train and was granted three seats. He had been an active Zionist most of his adult life, and this affiliation may have accounted for his selection. That commitment to Zionism—being on the Kasztner Train—may have saved our lives. Aunt Margalit and cousin Nomi, wife and daughter of my father's brother Sanyi, also were on the train. Margalit and her family were active Zionists as well.

June 30, 1944, was the departure date, but the group had to report to a designated assembly point, the Wechselmann Institute, a few days earlier. This large facility with spacious grounds, located on Columbus utca, previously had been used as a home for the blind and deaf. It was sufficiently large to accommodate the entire Kasztner train group.

I did not understand why we had to go there, but I had learned not to argue with my parents. Inside the Columbus utca facility, we encountered more people than I had ever seen before. I was disappointed when we found sleeping space only on the floor of a basement gymnasium. There were lots of people and lots of noise.

---

4   Randolph L. Braham, *The Politics of Genocide* (New York: Columbia University Press, 1981), 954.

We left the Wechselmann Institute for the railroad station as scheduled, on June 30. In preparing for the upcoming train ride out of our overcrowded home, we thought we were going to a neutral country, most likely Spain or Portugal. It was a warm June in Budapest and likely even warmer in Madrid or Lisbon. Aware that neither I nor my parents spoke Spanish or Portuguese, I wondered how quickly we'd gain fluency in a new language and how we'd manage until we did.

But that was a worry for another day. We packed for warm weather and mostly took what the Nazis ordered us to take: A limited number of changes of clothing, all lightweight, were delineated in a packing list the Nazis provided.

We optimistically walked to the Rákos utca railroad station in Budapest. It was a hot day, and our luggage was heavy, but there had not been an air raid that day, and we encountered no obstacles on the way to the railroad station.

Decades later, during one of our daily walks in Overland Park, Kansas, in the late 1990s, my father told me more about packing for the train ride. The packing instructions from the Nazis had included food in general, but not the type or quantity. Aware that cooking oil has a high caloric content, my parents had decided to take along a jug of oil. The oil was both heavy and messy. A group of chalutzim on the street offered to trade the oil for some other food items. (Chalutzim were a group of generally young men, along with women—chalutzot—who were pioneers, planning to go to Palestine to work the land agriculturally.) My parents accepted the offer, and I don't believe they ever regretted the exchange.

In the absence of guards or troops around the outside of the train station, we headed for the entrance without incident. I was mindful of my parents' admonitions about drawing attention to myself and was somewhat fearful, but I also thought that the Nazis couldn't be so terrible after all if they were letting us leave. So I was optimistic about the train ride. We were leaving behind the war and, with it, Nazi atrocities. I didn't know what was really happening and most likely neither did my parents. Auschwitz, Buchenwald, and Bergen-Belsen were faraway places with no particular connotations one way or the other.

Our welcome at the station turned out to be a foreshadowing of what was to come. A group of malevolent, uniformed Nazis was stationed just inside the station door. Impeccably attired, they presented a sharp contrast to our disheveled and unkempt appearance. The Wechselmann Institute collection facility provided no showers, and we had neither bathed nor changed our clothes since leaving our home. The insulting language began at the door. A Fräulein, during an earlier and less traumatic time, had taught me a little German. The abusive language I heard was only vaguely familiar, but the tone of voice and accompanying body language clearly indicated the essence of the Nazi message. Cowering in fear, my parents and I stopped. We had no idea where to go next.

An approaching Nazi directed us to our train, which was not close by. We passed two or three Jewish women with whom my parents had been acquainted. They were handwashing some Nazis' clothes in small basins in the railroad station—a strange sight. I asked my parents about this, and they could not (or would not) give me an answer.

We approached a cattle car with no visible passengers. All the doors seemed closed. As my mother told me years later—still in search of our train—closer to the car she heard pounding on the side walls of the wagons with muffled cries of desperate human beings yelling, "Help. Help. Water. Water." My mother said we all averted our eyes and kept on walking. By this time, we had been told by other Jews that offering help to anyone was hopeless.

We finally reached a long cattle train and learned it was there for us. These were not the passenger cars we had expected to find, ready to take us to Spain or Portugal. It was a train designed to transport animals, and we were driven inside like a herd. The Nazis jammed as many as 60 or more humans into each car. There was no room to lie down, and barely enough space to sit. On that stifling day in June 1944, there was but one grated opening, perhaps 12 inches square, as the sole source of ventilation for the entire car. Once the doors were closed, the inside quickly became unbearable. The Nazis provided no food or drink initially and gave us one bucket for human waste that was emptied from time to time. We would ultimately be on that train for nine days.

There were 1,684 people on the cattle train. They included the ultraconservative, anti-Zionist Satmars led by Rebbe Joel Teitelbaum. My father belonged to the Macabbea, the university Zionist organization, which had many members who had formed decades-long friendships. My parents knew many Zionists and identified with that group. The Zionists' goal was to make aliyah from a seaport near the train's destination in Spain or Portugal. There were rich Jewish businessmen in the group, and many teachers, as well as professionals representing most walks of life.

There were 35 cars on the train. My parents told me the leadership, including Rezső Kasztner's close and extended family as well as some of their friends, traveled in a little more comfort than the rest of us did. They were assigned one boxcar just for family and friends. A few of the cars apparently carried luggage. I don't know how much, if any, of our luggage was transported in the luggage cars. I sat on the floor, supported by my father's suitcase. I had to curl up my legs because there was insufficient room to extend them.

Though my parents were acquainted with many of our fellow passengers, I was not. My Aunt Margalit Gondos and my first cousin Nomi Gondos were members of our group, as were our family friends Janos, Erzsi, and their daughter Bori, from Budapest, but they were not in our cattle car. I was excited when I saw Bori and immediately wanted to arrange time together. Bori and her parents were less enthusiastic and suggested that we wait. For some inexplicable reason, she and I no longer seemed to be friends.

With everyone on board, the train began to move, and many passengers expressed doubts about our proposed destination. The small children were hot and tired, and most made their feelings known. Some older passengers began to complain, and multiple sounds of "oy vey" could be heard. I didn't fully understand what was happening, but I became apprehensive as well. Access to an outside view was very limited, and my parents were as uninformed as the rest. They had studied European geography and knew that Spain and Portugal were southwest of Budapest—but judging by the rising and the setting of the sun, they concluded we were headed northwest.

Soon our train began to go straight north, and there were more sounds of "oy vey" throughout the cars. A railroad station sign appeared on the horizon, and we quickly learned, much to our dismay, that we were arriving in Linz, Austria. Linz is in northern Austria, not on the way to Spain or Portugal. At the sound of air raid sirens, the train stopped. Harried Nazi personnel drove us off the train, telling us to stay still. They then disappeared.

Though no one mentioned escape, I thought an opportunity to escape had presented itself and wondered why no one had seized it. My seven-year-old mind assumed that escaping would solve all of our problems. Of course, I had not considered that escapees needed some place to go and a safe way to get there. No one had explained to me that all undocumented persons found on the streets were arrested, and, depending on who they were, shot. We were a sorry-looking group, and our identities as Jews would not have been a secret for long. If not executed on the spot, we would surely have been deported to the nearest gas chambers. Escape may have been tempting, but the chances of success were remote. Our group stood quietly until the all-clear siren about a half hour later, at which time the guards reappeared, and the chance for escape had passed.

Brandishing whips and machine guns, the Nazis ordered us in abusive language to start walking. Even though stretching our legs was welcome, we were hungry and dehydrated, and the walk was unpleasant. Ultimately we arrived at a low industrial building and were herded inside. Men and women were marshaled into separate lines. There were two Nazis heading the women's line.

One clearly outranked the other. A third Nazi with shears and razor in hand was ready for work. The ranking Nazi whispered directions to his underling, who relayed the information to the barber. Thus began the head-shaving of the women. My Aunt Margalit, near the front of the line, screamed, "My hair, my hair, my beautiful hair!" as her head was shaved. About a dozen women had already lost their hair when a messenger ran into the cavernous space and whispered in the ear of the ranking officer. The officer transmitted the information to his underling, and the head shavings stopped. My mother and I were near the end of the line. With so many women ahead of us, we never fully realized the fate that awaited us until the threat had passed.

The Nazi guards chastised us for our filthy state. We certainly were dirty, but how could we be otherwise? We had been confined inside a hot and congested train for days, with no sanitary facilities of any sort. They told us we would be cleansed and deloused. I had never heard the latter term and was confused. My mother did not explain. We were driven, again with multiple insults, into another cavernous space with hundreds of overhead showers. I didn't understand at the time that some adults were aware that overhead showers controlled by Nazis sometimes dispensed gas, not water. The Nazis ordered us to undress and to place our belongings on peripheral benches. I had never undressed in front of strangers and certainly not soldiers. I complained, but my mother said to do as I was told.

We all stood under the shower heads as warm water came out. I considered the showers to be pleasant, but I suspect many of the adults were simply relieved to have had no terrible surprises in that room. Afterward, we were instructed to get dressed and return to our cattle train.

The train moved in a northwesterly direction, and everything began to change. Evergreens were the predominant vegetation, and people wore heavier clothes than we had seen earlier. The scenery was refreshing, with the tall trees providing abundant shade. Later, when the train stopped, we could see this certainly was not Spain or Portugal.

We had become accustomed to threats and verbal abuse and even expected it when encountering our captors. However, the Nazis at the station were more vicious than anyone with whom we had previously engaged. A group of sinister, malevolent uniformed men, again holding whips and machine guns, awaited us. The screaming of obscenities began even before we left the cattle cars. "You pigs. You vermin. You worthless beings. Get off the train and line up," they yelled. Brandishing their weapons, they provided no opportunity for us to deviate from their commands.

When all passengers were outside, the Nazis ordered us to march in formation. We were accompanied by a large group of uniformed SS soldiers. A few were on foot, some in cars, others on horseback, and one or two on motorcycles. The yelling and intimidation continued. Over 1,600 tired, hungry, and dehydrated souls were driven along the road like a herd of cattle. It had been nine days since we left Budapest.

Carrying our meager belongings, we walked for a long time, seemingly hours. The verbal abuse intensified whenever a member of the group slowed down. Eventually we reached a dirt road, and minutes later we arrived at a compound surrounded by electrified barbed wire. The gate was open and we went through it. There were multiple guard towers on the perimeter, all fully staffed. A wide dirt area divided the camp into two sections, men on one side, women and children on the other. The Nazis announced we had arrived at the Bergen-Belsen concentration camp.

They provided some information prior to assigning us to our barracks, though I can't recall how the barrack assignments were determined. First, they emphasized that attempts to escape were futile because landmines surrounded the camp. Second, mandatory outdoor roll call, or "appell," would take place every morning. Third, we were not permitted to leave our barracks during the night. There may have been more information, but I did not hear, or grasp, the rest.

We arrived in Bergen-Belsen on July 9, wearing the same clothes we had worn when we left Budapest on June 30. My mother and I were assigned to barrack 11-Z, a noisy, congested, unventilated space. I recall no food or drink being provided that evening, and there was no possibility to wash. We were allowed a trip to the latrine. Hot, tired, and hungry, we went to bed.

CHAPTER 6

Bergen-Belsen

Morning came early in our barrack. Our bunks, three high and three abreast, were too small even for the children. There were no mattresses, just dirty blankets and layers of filthy straw. The straw was a breeding ground for a variety of vermin, many of which had feasted on our limbs all night long.

No wonder we were relieved to get up in the morning. The children competed for the distinction of having the most bites. The kid with the greatest number was champion of the day. There were no prizes or special privileges, but there were accolades from the other children. Occasionally an adult provided input, but a child who could identify sources of the bites was considered a hero. We were aware of bedbugs, fleas, and rodents, but mostly we didn't know what had bitten us.

Close to 100 women and children were housed in our barrack. With the back and front doors shut, there was no ventilation, and the summer heat was stifling.

If the heat and the uncomfortable accommodations didn't wake us up, the young children or their biologic needs did. We were forbidden to leave the barrack after lights out. The single toilet in the rear of the barrack rarely functioned. It was either stopped up or overflowing. As a result, mothers devised creative versions of chamber pots, made of containers large enough to hold a night's output. Sometimes one chamber pot served several family members, or even more than one family. Leaks and breaks were common. Typically, long before sunrise, little kids began their pleas to use the chamber pots. Odors from the overflowing toilet coupled with the leaky makeshift chamber pots permeated barrack 11-Z.

Our food rations were very limited. I have no idea whether the more religiously observant in the group adhered to the laws of kashrut, the kosher dietary laws, though it hardly mattered. Our rations contained no meat.

Food delivery came twice a day in a wooden cart. The deliverers must have been camp inmates, but not from our subcamp. Breakfast arrived early, before appell. The menu varied. There was always ersatz coffee—cold, weak, and tasteless, with neither milk nor sugar. Sometimes we were given a small amount of cold rice, while on other days we received a crust of dry bread. With eating and drinking utensils in hand, we lined up to receive our meals. My father estimated our daily food intake to be about 350 calories.

There were advantages to being near the head of the line. These included the possibility of receiving coffee that was not ice cold and never-warm-but-not-cold rice, and precluded the chance that food would run out before it was our turn. One time, my mother and I decided to save half of our breakfast for lunch. We feared that someone would steal the food but left it on the windowsill anyway. The containers were empty when we returned. The rice we had saved for later was not eaten by anyone we knew; the guilty parties were rodents. We never did that again.

The second meal of the day came in the afternoon. Generally, it consisted of an orangish, dishwatery liquid. The Nazis euphemistically called it soup. The "soup" sometimes contained pieces of turnip and, occasionally, a piece of potato. Potatoes were a rare delicacy. My mother always saved hers for my father and me.

We used eating utensils we had brought from Budapest, and we greatly valued them. And we learned the hard way that others valued them as well. One morning my mother couldn't find her cup and bowl. She looked everywhere and asked everyone, but the bowl and cup were nowhere to be found. This loss meant she could not collect her food rations, because the rule was "no utensils, no food." She was resigned to fasting that day. Walking through the barrack, my mother encountered Erzsi, an old friend from Budapest, who was carrying my mother's bowl and cup. Mother was surprised and asked her to return the eating utensils. Erzsi insisted they were, and had always been, her own property. After a very heated argument, Erzsi became agitated and threw the bowl and cup at my mother, saying, "These items have always been mine. However, you seem to need them more than I do." She then stalked off. This was a disturbing but not unusual incident. Our perceptions of morality, right or wrong, and consideration for others assumed new meanings in Bergen-Belsen. The importance of survival far outweighed any other values.

There was little to do in the camp. The weather was mild during our early weeks there, in July and August, and the lay leadership tried to keep us busy. Teachers, a profession well-represented in the camp, organized classes for the children. There were neither books nor other teaching materials, but there was a desire to teach, and many of the children wanted to learn. Classes met regularly during our early days in Belsen.

One of many well-respected Budapest teachers, Kudelka Rozsi, was my teacher. She must have been a Zionist, because the Zionist group had asked her to teach their children. We gathered daily for instruction, and I enthusiastically attended her classes. She was committed to diverting children's attention from the reality of our daily existence.

Though there were no books, Kudelka was undeterred. She instructed us verbally and quizzed her students to reinforce what had been taught. I was delighted to learn from the teacher's lectures. We worked on multiplication tables.

The classes continued to meet for weeks. Kudelka continued to teach even as we all became weak and apathetic, but as everything in our lives deteriorated and students were starving and sick, attendance dropped off. The class size dwindled day by day until there were only two or three of us left. I may have been the last of her students and finally had to drop out because I was starving. While they lasted, the classes were a challenging diversion from the Nazi atrocities that engulfed our lives.

All levels of Jewish observance existed in the camp, from the Satmar Chasidim at one end of the spectrum to the Zionists at the other end. The Orthodox, the status quo, and the Neologs were between the two. A schism within Hungary's Jewish community between 1869 and 1871 officially divided the community into two factions: the Orthodox and the Neolog. The Orthodox remained traditional. The Neologs adopted a reform ideology of Judaism and were the most modern and the most liberal group. A portion in the middle refused to affiliate with either faction. They are referred to as the status quo ante.[5]

I recall no Zionist-led services at Bergen-Belsen. I am certain my father, a very active Zionist, would have informed us if there were. The Zionists planned to make aliyah and were involved in meetings and planning groups. They were the least religiously observant in the camp. The children all admired the Zionist chalutzim and chalutzot because they were young, energetic, and full of life and spirit.

The Satmar Chasidim were sure God watched over them. They prayed Shacharit (morning prayers), Mincha (afternoon

---

5   *Encyclopaedia Judaica*, vol. 8 (Jerusalem: Keter Publishing House, 1978).

prayers), and Maariv (evening prayers) every day, convinced that God would protect them. Chasidim adhere to a strict, literal interpretation of the *Tanakh*, the Hebrew Bible. They consider all that happens in this world to be God's will. For them, Bergen-Belsen was a detour on the way to their God-determined destination. They believed that God would provide for their release, and they had complete faith in the final outcome.

Though the Orthodox prayed three times a day as well, the two other groups, status quo and Neolog, had no organized or visible services. Or perhaps I was just unaware of their activities.

Erev Rosh Hashanah, the Jewish New Year, occurred on September 17, a little over two months after our arrival in Belsen. By then, hunger, filth, and disease best described our state of being. There was no cheer, no uplifting moment, nothing to indicate to us that the Jewish year 5705 would be better than 5704.

We heard and occasionally observed nearby bombings. Rather than fear, evidence of proximal bombings elicited states of euphoria among some inmates. Bombings were signals that the Allies were aggressively trying to defeat the Nazis. If the Allies won, we might be freed. We learned, long after World War II, that American bombers struck German oil factories within five miles of Auschwitz, but Auschwitz itself was never bombed. There were occasional visitors from humanitarian organizations, and they may have brought news pertinent to us. Similarly, we observed no bombs striking within the Bergen-Belsen concentration camp.

With this as a background, I—a seven-year-old—desperately wanted to attend Rosh Hashanah services. I had heard after appell that services would be held, but not where or who would conduct them. I was oblivious to the differences among the Orthodox and Neolog. My friends and I discussed attending services, and I ran to ask my mother to take me. My mother—disheartened, emaciated, and weak after 14 weeks in Belsen—was lying on her back, eyes closed. Reluctant to disturb her, I softly asked if we could attend services. Receiving no reply, my request was more forceful the second time. Mother opened her eyes and, without facial expression, replied, "I don't want to go." I did not give up easily and began to beg. No success. I begged and cajoled, even cried. I must have worn her down, because she finally agreed to go. I was pleased, but not finished. My agenda contained a second item. I was anxious for us to get "all dressed up."

We had some good clothes in a suitcase under the bunks, and I thought we should wear them. My mother disagreed. She shook her head even before I finished asking. "Why bother? Why should we go to all that trouble when no one would care or even notice?" she said. "I don't care and neither does anyone else." I began to argue and plead. "We've not worn our good clothes since we left home. When will we have an opportunity to wear them again? Besides, this is a holiday. Please." Again, I argued and pleaded until she agreed to the makeover, probably out of a desire to be left alone. Mother did agree to dress up, but I had to promise to find the clothes and, after services, to put them back in the suitcase.

We pulled out the suitcase. Even to our uncritical eyes, the clothes were not nearly as good as we remembered. There were holes, probably chewed by rodents, and the garments appeared dirty and wrinkled. Nevertheless, we changed from our everyday rags into the better ones. Anyuka had a two-piece dress of brown georgette, piped in beige at the neck, sleeves, and in the front. The front of my thin wool burgundy dress was smocked, and it had a sash and a white linen collar. I thought we both looked gorgeous.

Anyuka and I walked down the compound to services. I have no memory of the service or who conducted it, but I will always remember my feeling of elation, the psychological lift provided by the change in clothing. For that short time, I was transformed from a dirty, malnourished, concentration camp inmate to a glamorous, beautifully attired, fashionable young girl attending High Holiday services. I was celebrating Rosh Hashanah. I had not felt such pride since we arrived in Bergen-Belsen.

CHAPTER 7

Keeping Our Minds Busy

Though mental health was important, physical health was necessarily a more pressing concern. There were 1,684 inmates in our section of Bergen-Belsen, and thus 1,684 opportunities for infection and disease. The Nazis provided no medical care and no supplies or drugs of any sort. But as long as we followed their regulations, they did not interfere with intracamp matters. The most important Nazi dictates were daily attendance at appell and cooperative behavior while there. Additionally, we were ordered to keep our barracks clean, and we were forbidden to leave the barracks at night.

Presence of medical manpower compensated for our lack of medical supplies and prescription drugs. There were many well-trained medical specialists at the camp: a dermatologist, a pediatrician, and my father the radiologist, to name just a few. A small group, including my father, assembled every now and then to discuss topics of medical interest. Originally, the group's mission was to provide a semblance of human activity for the group.

As months passed and our physical conditions deteriorated, the doctors recognized that medical support would be available only through them. And they began to provide a modicum of medical care to the inmates by making themselves available for daily consultation in one of the barracks. Without equipment and drugs, their effectiveness was limited. However, sometimes their good advice was sufficient to make a difference. Providing even a limited amount of help served as a real morale-booster, not only to those in need of care but to the physicians themselves, restoring self-esteem and thereby some sense of humanity.

I had two occasions to consult the medical group and benefitted both times. The first problem was an infestation of warts on both hands. My father had no idea how to help me. He took me to see his friend, the dermatologist. The dermatologist seemed familiar with my problem. He explained that the highly contagious warts, verruca vulgaris, were caused by the human papilloma virus and were transmitted by casual skin contact. He postulated that eliminating the biggest warts would be a sufficient cure and that the others would recede on their own. He had no medical instruments and had to devise an alternative plan. He tied a very strong thread tightly around the base of the largest warts and instructed me to return the next day, at which time he tightened the thread. This was repeated over several days until the largest warts fell off. As he had suspected, within a week or so, all the warts were gone. The dermatologist and my family were delighted.

My second problem presented as multiple abscesses on both lower legs. My friends in the barracks and their mothers were mortified of spreading infections. They enthusiastically cheered me on as my parents sought medical help. Apuka believed that these furuncles were bacterial staphylococcus aureus infections caused by a dirty environment and poor general hygiene. I visited the medical clinic, and the doctors there confirmed the diagnosis. They knew what to do, but lacked the equipment to do so. Somehow they found a few sulfa pills and hoped they'd be useful. The team put out a call for needles, matches, alcohol, Vaseline, and bandages. Fellow inmates invested in my care as they sought to provide what needed materials they could. They responded with Vaseline, matches, and a needle, but nothing else was available.

My mother was instructed to take me to the washroom. With cold water and no soap, she scrubbed both legs and brought me back to the makeshift clinic. My father pulverized the sulfa pills and mixed them with the Vaseline, creating an ointment. A dermatologist sterilized the needle over a match flame and incised each of the abscesses. Having no available alcohol with which to disinfect my legs, the sulfa ointment was applied directly to the lesions. I was instructed to return the following day at which time the remainder of the ointment was applied. Within the next three days, the lesions disappeared, and my legs healed.

My cure was a camp event. The doctors were heroes. I was a celebrity, along with those who had participated. Briefly, we forgot our daily problems and were transformed into a group of human beings working toward a common cause.

The proceedings had a more lasting effect on my mother. Following the episode of filth-generated leg abscesses, Mother concluded that cleanliness was next to godliness and that enhanced efforts might avert such infections in the future. She was going to keep me clean no matter what. Bergen-Belsen provided neither soap nor hot water, but at the end of our compound there was a washroom containing huge gray laundry tubs. My mother took me to the washroom every day, where I was forced to strip and climb into a tub to be scrubbed from head to toe. This was fine in the summer, but it gets cold pretty early in northern Germany, and we had no heat. I don't recall any other children being subjected to daily scrubbings, but I do remember shivering and resisting without success.

There is no scientific way to judge the effectiveness of the daily scrubbings. It is true that I did not suffer from any more infections once my mother's efforts at cleanliness began. However, I don't know if I stayed healthy because of her or in spite of her.

We, the Hungarian inmates of Bergen-Belsen, were a pathetic lot by mid-fall of 1944. Our very meager food allotment had reduced most of us to walking skeletons. Close quarters and rampant bacterial and viral infections resulted in many sick inmates. The cruelty and dehumanization we experienced in Nazi hands caused widespread hopelessness. We had a past, an abominable present, and no perceived future. Living just one more day became the predominant goal and focus. Many, if not most, spent the majority of their days on their bunks, staring glassy-eyed at the ceiling. My mother was no exception.

Our status in Bergen-Belsen was unlike that of other concentration camp inmates. The Nazis had been promised a specific price to transport the Kasztner Train group to a neutral country. The down payment had been made, but there was a large balance due. Aware that our group had to be kept intact for them to collect the balance of the ransom, the Nazis allowed us some intracamp freedom and did not force us to work. The war was ending, and Hitler was willing to compromise his goal of killing all European Jewry in return for money. Although we did not have to work in the camp, starvation, disease, and psychological abuse took a heavy toll.

Mother was a pragmatic person, generally a hopeful realist. A manifestation of that personality trait resurfaced one early fall day as she recognized the contagion of hopelessness. She was determined to lift the spirits of as many children as she could, including her own.

Having studied art and design, Anyuka decided to teach art to any interested children. My mother announced her intentions just after appell. A handful of kids showed up at our barracks at the appointed time. There were no art supplies, so my mother improvised. Using the dirt at her feet as a sketchpad and a stick instead of a drawing pencil, she showed the children how to draw beautiful things like butterflies and flowers, none of which were to be seen in Bergen-Belsen. The children were very responsive and proudly shared their masterpieces within a half hour. Another class was planned for the following day. The sounds of happy childhood chatter and giggles were heard as the kids returned to their barracks. My mother's spirits were also lifted, if only temporarily.

Other adults also sought ways to keep hope alive. The Kasztner Train group had been organized mostly by Zionists as a vehicle to escape the Nazis and to make aliyah. The group expanded to include a variety of other Jews who had their own agendas that did not necessarily include going to Palestine. The Zionists, however, never wavered in their plan to make aliyah. The planning and organizing continued even behind the electrified barbed wire encircling the camp. There were committees covering all aspects of their goal.

As a seven-year-old, I was neither considered a prospective helper nor a significant decision-maker. However, I did observe the flurry of activity. In retrospect, the Zionist adults must have been aware of the seeming hopelessness of our situation. Discussing what would happen in Eretz Yisrael was positive, an affirmation of hope and humanity.

The residents of our barrack were a diverse group in terms of geographic origin, nationality, education, and socioeconomic levels. There were Hungarians and Romanians, people from big cities and small shtetls, the rich and poor, those who were uneducated and those who had PhDs. None of these designations seemed significant after a while; they were erased after a few months at the camp. What we all had in common was the only significant thing: the desire to live another day.

The women in 11-Z often sat in a circle on the floor. They

did not discuss world events, Jewish philosophy, or music. They often talked about what they would do after gaining their freedom. Some planned to visit new places or people. Others hoped to resume their previous lives, while still others did not know.

What they planned to cook in the future was another frequent conversation topic. Interestingly, though many of the ladies were familiar with gourmet cooking, they did not dream about sophisticated French pastries or coq au vin. Their cooking plans—their hopes, really—were to prepare *filling* dishes. They talked of Székely gulyás (Hungarian goulash), töltött paprika (Hungarian stuffed peppers), and other filling, high-calorie dishes and bread—always, bread. These wishes, of course, reflected our states of starvation.

I occasionally listened to these discussions and was amazed by the things I heard. On one occasion, the women discussed furs they had owned during an earlier time. Budapest was cold in the winter, and my mother had owned more than one fur coat. As far as I could determine, she wore furs to keep warm. I was surprised to hear about the multiple furs many of the other women had owned. Retrospectively, the furs increased in number and rarity as the conversations proceeded.

These acts of psychological resistance may seem inconsequential, but they were a lifeline for the sick and helpless inmates in the Bergen-Belsen camp. For the brief periods they lasted, they diverted us from Nazi cruelty, starvation, and hopelessness and provided a positive focus, in spite of our misery.

There were times when an unannounced Nazi or two came to inspect us and our barrack. Invariably, they declared the living space to be too filthy and added that we were "untermenschen"—subhuman. Our superior captors, they continued, soon would end our worthless lives. Needless to say, these visits amplified our devastation. We saw no hope.

The men's barracks were separate from the women's. Although women were permitted in the men's barracks, men could not enter ours. My father was emaciated and weak during the fall of 1944, and we did not see him often. I repeatedly asked to visit, but my mother consistently refused to take me. I have no idea what triggered her change of heart, but one afternoon she announced we were going to visit him. As we went through the doors of the men's barrack, I thought we had entered another world. There were no children there, and it was very quiet. There was soft lighting, and a few women, some of whom I recognized, were walking to and fro. They were "dressed up," actually less disheveled than we were.

We encountered a woman who lived in Barrack 11-Z. She was wearing makeup and a seemingly nice outfit of white pants and shirt. I said hello but was completely ignored. I complained to my mother, who refused to explain. Mother and I walked through the barrack and found my father lying on his low bunk. He smiled as we approached, and we had a pleasant conversation. He and mother exchanged a few words in hushed tones and then it was time to leave. In retrospect the men's barrack makes sense, but I had no idea what I was witnessing at the time.

Weeks, then months passed. Our environment was mostly

unchanged, but we inmates were physically deteriorating. Some children mingled and occasionally devised games to play, but most of the adults spent their days flat on their backs, apathetically staring at the ceiling.

Winter sunset came early in northern Germany. We had nothing to engage us and no energy or desire to be engaged. We went to sleep soon after sunset to awaken early the next day to clean the barracks, to ready us for impromptu inspections. Then we lined up for breakfast. We cleaned up after that, then we were assembled for appell.

Appell was our only consistent daily activity. We lined up outdoors shortly after breakfast, though the Nazis came at their own convenience. We stood outside, near our barracks, sometimes for hours at a time, in good weather and bad, in rain and snow, when it was warm and when the temperature was below freezing. It seemed like the weather in northern Germany was always unpleasant. We had been sufficiently intimidated to limit our conversation, because we feared being severely reprimanded.

Standing among the mass of dehumanized inmates, all expressionless and meek, I wondered about other people, those who were not in concentration camps. Did they engage in pleasant activities? Were their stomachs full? Did they have warm clothes in the winter? Did they do what they wanted, or were their lives structured by rules?

During the early months of our incarceration, while the weather was tolerable, the children played games while awaiting the Nazis. In order to avoid suspicion, we had to be very creative in finding games that required little overt action and that were easily terminated. "Telephone" met these criteria. One child would "call" another, transmit a brief story, and that child, in turn, would tell another. It was fun to see how the story changed as it was told and retold. We often played the game, our voices dropping to whispers as soon as we saw Nazis approaching.

Our captors appeared in groups to count us. Dressed immaculately, with boots as shiny as mirrors and knife-edged pant creases, they brandished their weapons to intimidate us, their helpless victims. Though I don't recall physical abuse, we were always frightened. Nasty and intimidating, their tirades were menacing. They threatened to kill us, to maim us, and to starve us. They told us we were worthless vermin who did not deserve to live and that they planned to cleanse the world of filth like us. The Nazis never failed to mention that we were "untermenschen," subhuman. I was seven at the time and was unaware of its definition. Some of my friends, more worldly than I, explained what it meant. I then began to wonder whether or not I was subhuman. After all, those in charge so often told me so.

Early in the Holocaust, my mother had instilled in me the importance of not attracting attention. She emphasized that I should never make eye contact with the enemy. The ranking Nazi soldier in the "inventory crew" was fair-haired, light skinned, tall, and slim. There was a long scar on his right cheek, extending at an angle, upward from his lip. I knew he was our captor, a ruthless individual. Nevertheless, I looked up to him and hoped he would notice me. In spite of my mother's admonitions, I tried to attract his attention with eye contact. Fortunately, I was unsuccessful in this.

Our clothing was inadequate for the brutal winter of northern Germany. Having been instructed to pack for a warmer climate, few in the group had coats or sturdy shoes. My shoe soles had become tissue-paper thin. My parents bartered some of their very meager food rations for a pair of high-heeled, oversized women's sandals. These were tied to my feet with twine, on top of what was left of my shoes. Walking in them was difficult, but they served their purpose: They prevented my feet from freezing. Mother and Father exchanged additional food rations for a scrap of blanket. They rolled it around me and fastened the end with a safety pin. I looked like a barrel, but it did keep me warmer during appell. By bartering away food on my behalf, my parents of course had even less to eat than before.

Mrs. Rosenberg, a seemingly healthy elderly woman with an orthopedic handicap, was allowed to stay inside during appell. She was also empowered to decide who was sick enough to stay indoors. As the one in charge of determining who could avoid exposure to the elements during appell, we admired and respected her. Being a friend of Mrs. Rosenberg was a coveted status that I never managed to achieve. Her rewards for this responsibility included a real cot near the door and the use of an adjacent table.

The indoor inventory crew differed from the group that counted us outside. An elderly Nazi, gruff but not outwardly hostile, came daily to count sick inmates in Barrack 11-Z. Actually, he never counted them. He and Mrs. Rosenberg had a friendly chat, followed by her report of the numbers. The elderly Nazi accepted her count and transmitted it to the tall blond soldier in charge. The tall blond Nazi usually did not question the tabulation.

We always worried that the count would not match expectations. On such occasions, the inventory count was repeated, sometimes several times, until the expected numbers were reached. Some in the barrack questioned the propriety of Mrs. Rosenberg's friendship with the Nazi. Did she, or someone else, compensate him for the special privileges she received? My mother considered such allegations to be idle gossip and thought Mrs. Rosenberg was just doing her job.

The number of infirm inmates always swelled on cold and wet days, giving the Nazi in charge an opportunity to scream, insult, and threaten those who remained indoors.

Daily appell was our source of news and an opportunity for the Nazis to announce changes in daily routine. Specifically, one very cold and wet day in late fall, they voiced objections to the number of people who stayed indoors when sick and therefore took advantage of the Nazis' kind and liberal gesture. They threatened to force all inmates to attend outdoor appell if the practice did not stop. Around that time, the elderly Nazi, Mrs. Rosenberg's "friend," stopped coming. It's possible he was reassigned or had retired, or even died. We never found out. His replacement was as malevolent as the worst of his Nazi colleagues, and the liberal evaluation of who was or was not sick stopped. Mrs. Rosenberg, who still managed to stay indoors during appell, was stripped of her powers. You had to be gasping for your last breath to stay inside after that.

"Our fate in Bergen-Belsen will be announced at appell," my father insisted. Therefore, every day without an announcement was a good day. Another day to live.

Being able to stay with my parents during the Holocaust may have been the primary factor in assuring my relative well-being. My parents were smart, goal-oriented people who did what was necessary. Many other children my age were separated from their families, cast adrift without the physical or emotional ability to deal with being alone. They faced unfamiliar, often tragic circumstances for which they were unprepared. With no preparation or experience, they had no idea how to deal with the consequences of these circumstances.

As time passed, our malnutrition worsened. Activities of any sort were now impossible. As we grew more emaciated, weak, and despondent, our despair hung over the Bergen-Belsen camp. It was December, with the dreadful weather exacerbating our declining physical state and low morale.

We often heard airplanes overhead and saw the flares of bombs dropping, re-enforcing the likelihood that the Axis was losing the war. Even though such events gave us some hope, we feared our ability to survive concentration camp conditions much longer.

CHAPTER 8

Switzerland

December 3, 1944, began as another miserable morning. As we struggled to warm up without blankets, warm clothes, or a heat source, a member of our camp leadership entered the barrack with the following announcement: "Be ready to leave Bergen-Belsen in two hours."

Our barrack came to life. Women scurried to find their suitcases and to pack whatever belongings they still owned. My mother and I pulled our suitcase from under the bunk, laid it on the pile of dirty straw, and began to pack. We had far less to pack than when we came. Perishable food had been consumed long ago. Disposable items were no longer there, and much of our clothing had either worn out or been lost.

We gathered our worn and dirty belongings and placed them inside the luggage. I had a book or two and my beloved doll, Zsuzsi. Zsuzsi was not packed, but everything else was.

With our coats (or coat substitutes), we stood near our bunks and luggage. Two hours passed, then three, four, five, and six. The regular watery tasteless soup was delivered in the evening along with news that our departure had been postponed until the following day. A similar experience happened the next day. Finally, on the third day, two days after the announcement of our departure, we left the Bergen-Belsen concentration camp.

The group left through the same gate we had entered five and a half months earlier, and we received marching orders similar to the ones given to us on arrival. However, this time we were accompanied by only a small group of Nazis. They did not order us to march in formation, and our guards actually seemed disinterested in the whole process. The weather was cold, and the road was icy. We walked, carrying our belongings, until we came to a train station, the same station at which we had arrived the preceding summer.

There, waiting for us, was a passenger train. This was the kind of train we had originally envisioned in Budapest. Infinitely better, this was a train designed and built for humans, not cattle. The Nazis ordered us to climb inside and find seats, which we eagerly did. The train began to move, but we were given no idea of our destination. The trip is a blur except for the food we were provided: sardines and chocolate. I hate sardines and am not enamored with chocolate. Nevertheless, at that time and in that place, both tasted better than anything I had ever eaten. The train left the Bergen-Belsen station near midnight on December 5, 1944.

I recall neither air raid sirens nor stops. We had traveled some distance when, unexpectedly, the train did stop. Looking out the window we saw a man in civilian clothes approaching the train. He was carrying a large suitcase. We observed another man, in German army uniform, approaching from the opposite direction. They met in the middle. The civilian passed the suitcase to the uniformed Nazi, and each went back to his place of origin.

Later, when we were safely out of Nazi clutches, my parents explained what had happened. The train had stopped at the Swiss–German border. Saly Mayer, the Swiss Jewish representative of the American Jewish Joint Distribution Committee, a leading global Jewish humanitarian organization, came from the Swiss side. He carried a suitcase containing the remaining part of the bribe Kasztner had negotiated with Adolf Eichmann. Klaus Becher, the uniformed Nazi from the other side, was there to collect the balance of the ransom. Mayer passed the suitcase to Becher, and each man returned to his respective country. My parents believed the promise of that ransom money helped keep us alive during our time in Bergen-Belsen. My father always said that even the Nazis had their price.

The train moved on after the exchange. We saw a well-illuminated town and heard the welcoming sound of church bells. Being Jewish, I had never in the past responded to their sound. On that particular occasion, it was the most beautiful music possible. The sound of church bells reflected peace and joy.

We disembarked in St. Gallen, Switzerland, on December 7, 1944. Welcoming words, most likely from representatives of the International Red Cross, greeted us as we left the train on Swiss soil. The Swiss ushered us into a nearby auditorium-like space that contained tables set with dishes, silverware, and napkins. We sat down at our hosts' invitation and were served a filling meal. There were several courses, and seconds, even thirds, were offered. When our stomachs were full, we were directed to an adjacent room where hundreds of mattresses, outfitted with pillows and blankets, had been set up. We lay down, and I promptly went to sleep. A sumptuous breakfast awaited us the following morning before we were directed to the train that would take us farther into Switzerland.

The ride was wonderfully scenic. Switzerland is a beautiful country. We saw mountains, rivers, and lakes. We transferred to buses near Montreux and, not much later, we arrived at a scenic spot high up in the mountains. We saw beautiful Lake Geneva down below and several tourist hotels nearby. We were in Caux sur Montreux. Hotel Esplanade was the largest hotel in Caux, and a significant part of our group was assigned there. My parents and I were sent to the Hotel Beau Site, where we were accommodated in a nice single room with its own bath.

At first the Kasztner Train group was housed together, but after the war's end, the group dispersed. About 700 of the group made their way to Palestine. A few hundred returned to Hungary, and some went to other countries.

For us, the early and mid-1940s had been a time of misery, fear, cruelty, uncertainty, loss, and disappointment. In Switzerland in late 1944, there was no more cruelty. The Swiss neither physically abused nor starved us. They fed us adequately, provided decent housing and medical care, and gave us a limited amount of freedom.

Uncertainty, however, prevailed. We were no longer inmates in a concentration camp, but Switzerland was merely a temporary stop. Where would we go next? Could or should we go back to Budapest? To Palestine? To America? Somewhere else? What would we do once we were there? Would there be a means of support? We had no idea about our options, or even if we had any. We had heard nothing about my parents' families. Had they been deported? Were they still alive? Were they ill? These questions dominated our lives during the early months in Switzerland. Such issues commonly do not confront children of seven or eight; playdates and school are more common topics. But Switzerland was not our home, and the usual concerns of childhood were still subject to wartime restrictions and the trauma we had endured at the hands of the Nazis. I loved and missed my grandparents, but I wished we occasionally could focus on something else, something I wanted to do. I had missed out on so much of childhood that I was forgetting how to play. I wished for a playdate with a girlfriend, a chance to play house with my doll. I just didn't want to be growing up so fast.

As Zionists, my parents had planned to emigrate to Palestine. There were incessant committee meetings about plans for the group's future there. My father enthusiastically participated in all aliyah-related activities in Switzerland. The group organized an immersion camp for Palestine-bound children in Bex, and my parents enrolled me.

Bex, a small, scenic, and heavily forested community in southwest Switzerland, was the campsite. It was equipped with tents and shaded wooden picnic tables. The tables served as both school desks and dining tables. Each of the large tents accommodated several children.

Devorah, my Hebrew teacher, was a curly-headed young chalutzah in her late teens or early twenties. She was lively, fun, and kind. Devorah taught conversational Hebrew at our daily sessions around the picnic table. She gave us each a small notebook for vocabulary lists. Some students quickly lost theirs, and Devorah graciously replaced them. I proudly bragged that I still had my notebook. But by the time my notebook did disappear, Devorah had no more replacements. She was unable to give me a new one, and I had no place to record my newly learned vocabulary. I complained and cried, but to no avail. I was convinced that Devorah disliked me.

An ugly rash and scabs surfaced over my upper lip. Instinctively, I recognized it to be a problem, and I tried to keep others from noticing. The strategy worked for a day or two until the visiting mother of one of my tent mates saw the lesions and announced I had impetigo. The lady was a self-proclaimed cosmetologist and was certain of her diagnosis. I did not know what a cosmetologist was, and I had never heard of impetigo. It was contagious, I learned. Alarm soon permeated the camp and, for the sake of other campers, I was sent to a nearby hospital.

They placed me in a large children's ward. Everyone spoke a foreign language I could not identify. (Since Bex was in the French sector of the country, I now realize that the language must have been French.) The staff treated my impetigo, but they made no effort to communicate or to put me at ease. I was isolated and lonely and was disappointed that my parents did not visit.

Paul, a teenaged visitor who spoke Hungarian, appeared on my second or third day in the hospital. I didn't know why he had come or who had sent him, but his kindness was welcome. He knew my name and why I was hospitalized. Paul seemed to be fluent in French and advocated for me with the staff. He repeatedly asked if I was feeling better and how he could help me. He visited two or three times. Slowly, I recovered.

During Paul's final visit he indicated he would join me as I traveled back to Caux sur Montreux to join my parents. Together, we left the hospital and rode a bus up the mountainside. My parents and I had hiked around there, and I recognized the area. I informed Paul I could find my way back to the Hotel Beau Site. We said goodbye and I got off the bus. I walked for a while, approached the hotel, and went inside to find my parents. They were surprised to find me at their door. Apparently, they had not been notified of my release.

Great news arrived on May 8, 1945—VE Day, officially marking the end of World War II. We had been on our daily hike that afternoon as group after group approached us and told us things in a language we couldn't understand. Everyone we met seemed happy, elated even. Finally some German speakers came down the mountain and shared the good news: "The war was over." My parents were excited, and we quickly returned to our hotel to learn more.

News began to flow with the end of hostilities, and news about fellow Jews started to arrive. Communication was slow, as Europe was in great disarray in 1945, but our leadership posted lists of survivors as well as lists of victims as soon as they were available. These lists were compiled by the Red Cross, Jewish communal organizations, and international humanitarian groups, among others. Some lists contained only names of survivors, while others named their locations as well. Lists of victims were always separate. My parents rushed to examine the newest postings and spent hours searching for familiar names. Weeks passed and there were none. The uncertainty continued.

Margalit and Nomi Gondos, my aunt and cousin, had been with us in Bergen-Belsen and came with the group to Switzerland. Sanyi Gondos, my uncle, had been conscripted into the Hungarian Labor Service before our deportation, and no one had heard from him. Margalit, convinced she was destined to reconnect with her husband in Budapest, arranged transportation to go home. Much to our surprise, but not to hers or her husband's, Uncle Sanyi was waiting for her in their apartment when she arrived.

We had no one with whom to connect in Budapest, and so we waited. News of gas chambers and crematoria were widely disseminated, but still no family names appeared on the multitude of posted lists. The Red Cross tried to help, but they had no information for us.

My parents ultimately reconnected with a few surviving distant relatives in Hungary. They had no specific information but confirmed what my parents had feared: that many of our family members had been deported to death camps and had not returned.

How does one process the annihilation of an entire family? Throughout the Nazi occupation of Pest, the hell of Bergen-Belsen, and our first few months in Switzerland, we had hoped to be reunited with family. Such hope provided strength and purpose. Little by little we realized that our family was lost. My parents were devastated. Their hopes had been shattered.

We learned, many years later through the International Red Cross, that much of my mother's family was murdered in the Auschwitz gas chambers on June 30, 1944, the date we had boarded the train in Budapest for Bergen-Belsen. Laci, my mother's brother, had been conscripted into the Labor Service. We understand his battalion was lost in the battle of Don River, Saguenay, near Voronezh, Russia, in January of 1943. Pircsi, his wife, was deported to Auschwitz, transferred to Bergen-Belsen, and then died of tuberculosis in Sweden after the war.

Our lives in Bergen-Belsen had been tightly controlled but uncomplicated. We were served food at predictable times, lined up for appell when commanded to do so, and regularly cleaned our barracks. Otherwise, there was little we had to do. Real life, with its challenges and disappointments, resurfaced in Switzerland. My parents faced the tragedy of family members killed by the Nazis, but now they also had to deal with an uncertain future. Hungarians were complicit in the murder of over 450,000 Jews. We would not return to Hungary. But where would we go? Where *could* we go?

Zoltan and Margaret Gondos, my aunt and uncle in Arlington, Virginia, encouraged us to join them there. Zoltan, my father's brother, had gone to medical school in Bologna, Italy, and moved to the US in 1938. Margaret, Zoltan, and their son, Gordon, provided much-needed emotional and financial support for us. Two other, more distant family members also helped us financially. Sandor Kohn was the brother of my mother's second cousin, Piri. Sandor and his wife, Erna, had escaped from the Nazis to Scotland, where he changed his surname to Conn. Sandor Bleuer also loaned us money. This Sandor was my maternal grandmother's first cousin who lived in Bordeaux, France. (Later, after our arrival in the US and at Sandor's request, my parents repaid him with American truck tires, which they shipped to Bordeaux.)

Although my father had been committed to making aliyah, my mother, worn out by the struggles of recent years, sought only peace and family. After much soul-searching, they decided to come to America, aware that getting a visa would be a lengthy process.

The news that we would not make aliyah greeted me as I joined my parents after immersion camp in Bex. I had spent my early childhood in a Zionist home, left Budapest with a Zionist group. Aliyah had always been the family's stated goal. After Hebrew immersion program, I could not understand the choice of America over Palestine. At seven, I never questioned my parents' decisions. They had been the only stable force in my life, and I believed their judgment to be infallible. I believed what they believed. I had not been present for the discussions about America, and the decision was suddenly thrust upon me. I was puzzled, but I never verbalized objections.

The decision not to go to Palestine presented us with new problems. Where and how would we live until our visas arrived?

My father had not practiced medicine since the Nazi occupation of Budapest and feared he had lost some professional skills. He sought guidance from a colleague, a professor at the Zurich Medical School. The professor was involved in a research project and invited Bela to join him, without compensation, but this offer seemed the only way for my father's skills not to stagnate. There were now three apparent problems. First, how would the family get funds on which to live? Second, what about my mother? Third, what about Jutka? (My Hungarian nickname.)

My mother solved the first two challenges. She found a job peeling vegetables in the basement of the canton hospital in Zurich. (Swiss cantons are member states of the Swiss Confederation, analogous to individual states within the US.) Her meager compensation, including food for two, was just enough to rent a furnished room. My mother received a work permit, and she and my father received police permission to live in Zurich. The third problem was somewhat more challenging. What to do with an eight-year-old child?

The solution was to send me to boarding school. Where or how they heard of the school remains a mystery. My recollections reflect the perspective of a traumatized eight-year-old who had survived the horrors of Bergen-Belsen and then been separated from her parents. I was unaware of the realities my mother and father confronted in Switzerland.

The school, owned and directed by a German couple, had been established in Germany. The owners were not Nazis. They left Germany before World War II in order to avoid harassment, and they reestablished their school high in the Swiss Alps.

The directors seemed to spend little time together. The wife made no effort to befriend me. She occupied a small, well-furnished room in the school's main building and rarely joined us at communal meals, which were meager and generally not very good.

The husband with a Santa Claus-like beard also showed minimal interest in me. He occupied a large bedroom and listened to classical music at very high volume. He ate with the students and often made seemingly profound pronouncements in German. I spoke very little German upon arrival but gradually learned the language. After a few months I began to understand his words, though I was not inspired.

I arrived there in the summer of 1945. The setting was magnificent: A small shiny lake, in which I never swam, was surrounded by tall evergreens and majestic mountains. A lakeside chalet housed school headquarters. The back of the building had a panoramic view of nearby peaks.

A large commons room, adjoined by a kitchen and a laundry, occupied most of the lowest level. The commons room contained several long, rectangular tables with benches. It was used by the students three times a day for breakfast, dinner, and supper. There was a fireplace in one corner, with some upholstered easy chairs nearby, and a piano. Everything in the room was functional, but the furnishings were well worn, even shabby.

SWITZERLAND

The school espoused the benefit of work, and students were charged with doing necessary chores: cooking, cleaning, laundry, and some maintenance. I was assigned to the laundry, where my job was to sort and fold clothes. Between classes in the morning and housekeeping chores in the afternoon, there was limited opportunity to relax by the fire, and no one ever encouraged me to enjoy its warmth.

The student body was a mixed group. The youngest student was about six years old. He was a Swiss native. There were several 18-year-old students studying for their high school exams. A few were Swiss, and others were Jewish German refugees.

My best friend at school was Liesl, a Swiss girl my age. She was rumored to be incorrigible, having been expelled from more than one reform school. Liesl had a magnificent wardrobe: a red cape, red pants, and a red jacket. She and I often managed to entertain ourselves, though not necessarily according to the director's plans. Our favorite clandestine pastime was to wear costumes—usually one of Liesl's bright-red clothing items—and to pretend we were royalty, with Liesl as the reigning monarch. We played in our secret place, a hidden closet in our bedroom.

Another group of students included young teenaged boys, Jewish refugees, from Hungary. They had no interest in me. Hans and Erika, a brother and sister, were non-Jewish refugees from Alsace-Lorraine. Ilse, a Jewish German refugee whose father lived in the US, was awaiting a visa to join him. He sent her many packages containing clothes, books, and food. Ilse had a crush on Hans. He and his sister abused the friendship by "accepting" many of her gifts from America.

Classes, actually all instruction, were held in the mornings, often in beautiful outdoor settings. Although the school's location in the Swiss Alps was picturesque, its environment paralleled the frigid Alpine air. It was not a happy place.

As an eight-year-old I sought warmth and comfort, both of which were sadly lacking. My first teacher there reflected the general environment, and her classes were neither pleasant nor interesting. Fortunately, she left soon after my arrival and was replaced by a recent college graduate, Heidi. She was my favorite teacher, the only one I ever really liked. I believe my feelings were reciprocated.

Heidi was a large, blond-haired young woman with an ever-present smile and an engaging personality. We were instructed to call her by her given name, and she took an immediate interest in each of the six to eight students in the class. Learning became fun.

In warm weather, Heidi conducted classes in flower-covered meadows, and in winter she became our cross-country skiing instructor. In these informal settings we learned about plants, precipitation, mountains, and other things we encountered. Heidi was a great listener and encouraged all of us to share our thoughts with her, in and out of class.

Unfortunately for us, Heidi left after a few months when she found a job closer to her home.

An itinerant rabbi visited the school from time to time. He and I communicated in Hungarian, so I assume he came from Hungary. He must have taught Jewish history, Jewish religious customs, or conducted services. However, I recall only that he was my friend and always hugged and kissed me when he came. Unfortunately, he did not come often.

The owners wanted to increase enrollment, but to do so they needed more space. They acquired a larger multistory building in another canton. A bus moved the student body to the new site. Unlike the previous spot, the new location was not isolated. There was no lake, but we had a magnificent and unobstructed view of surrounding mountains. The school did have a swimming pool, but I never had the opportunity to swim in it.

The student body had changed before the move. My friend Liesl was gone, as were most of the Hungarian boys. My new roommates were two older girls who were unhappy to share their room with a nine-year-old. One evening as I tried to go to sleep, the girls in the room were noisy and refused to turn off the light. I repeatedly asked them to quiet down, and they ignored me. I threatened to complain, but the threat had no impact.

In desperation, I quietly approached the director's door and knocked. The volume on his gramophone was so high he did not hear my first few knocks. Ultimately, he opened the door and looked surprised to see me. He gruffly asked what I wanted and was completely disinterested in my complaint. I asked him two or three times to subdue my roommates, and he begrudgingly accompanied me back to my room. He very quietly and gently asked the girls to quiet down and then he left.

The director was annoyed to have been disturbed. The girls were amazed by my chutzpah, my nerve, and one of them slapped me on the face. They then resumed their loud, annoying activities.

Neither constant complaints to my parents, nor repeated requests to leave the school succeeded. Years later the Swiss government released documents about its wartime refugee population, which clarified some of my boarding school issues. As refugees, we were not free to move about the country. Everything we did, every move, required police permission, but police permission was not readily available. Not only did my parents lack the means to support me in Zurich, they did not have permission to take me there. As refugees at the mercy of the Swiss government, our options were severely limited. The boarding school may have been my parents' best—or possibly only—option.

In the spring of 1946 my father completed his share of the radiology research project in Zurich, and my parents were accepted to the Home for Intellectuals, Château de Frontenac in Geneva. My parents had to apply for admission to the home, but they neither told me about the criteria for acceptance nor the competitiveness of the applicant pool. Retrospectively, Home for Intellectuals may have been another name for Home for Professionals. They moved to Geneva, and I was overjoyed to join them there.

The château, a huge and stately place with enormous, beautifully landscaped grounds, contained multiple bedrooms, and most of the "intellectuals" were accommodated there. But, unfortunately, there was no available space when we arrived. The three of us were directed to a rental room at Madame Poulin's, whose apartment was nearby. We slept in our room but spent most of each day at the château.

There were approximately 30 "intellectuals" at the Château,

about 29 men and one woman. Though I recall interacting with Jews, there were non-Jews there as well. They spent their days studying, thinking, and writing. Though I have no specific recollections, my father was heavily involved in reading radiology literature, and I assume others also pursued their professional interests.

Occasionally the men shared ideas and accomplishments over dinner. The women, with the exception of the one intellectual woman, were charged with household chores. They cleaned, did laundry, and cooked. My mother was assigned to the meal preparation team. She planned tasty menus and became a very popular cook, in spite of having very limited cooking experience.

The intellectual woman, Dr. Emma Blau, became my tutor. A mathematician by profession but also fluent in English, she tutored me in both subjects. The fall of 1946 was supposed to be the beginning of my fourth-grade year at school. However, the war had robbed me of classroom time, and my parents feared I'd never catch up. Emma and I began daily sessions in late summer and continued meeting in the fall. She was a very demanding teacher, and she was very pleased with my accomplishments. Over several months, we developed mutual affection for one another.

Visas, with a finite life span, arrived in October. My parents immediately tried to book passage to America. They soon learned about a dock strike at US ports that had halted all boat traffic in both directions. They were determined not to allow our visas to expire, but there were no available tickets. Someone at Château de Frontenac suggested that our chances of booking passage to America would improve near a busy port. Without other options, my parents and I took a train to Genoa, Italy, on October 17, 1946, hoping to buy transatlantic tickets there. We stayed at a pensione, an Italian boarding house. One or sometimes both of my parents visited every travel and ticket agent in Genoa and took daily trips to the waterfront hoping to purchase tickets. Their initial searches for tickets were disappointing.

On our fourth day in Genoa, my mother returned to the pensione with exciting news: An empty coal freighter would soon be returning to the US. Instead of cargo, the ship's owners were willing to take 12 passengers. My parents rushed to buy tickets. It was October 21, and our departure was scheduled for the very next day. We sailed for America October 22, 1946.

CHAPTER 9

Embarking toward a New Life

The coal freighter *S.S. Matthew O'Brien*, owned by the Lykes shipping company, was a Liberty ship. Liberty ships were a class of simply and cheaply made cargo ships built within the Emergency Shipbuilding Program of World War II. Ours had been designed to carry coal and had been outfitted for a skeleton crew. Returning to the United States, the ship had no cargo because of a dock workers' strike. As a result, the shipping company agreed to use available cabins to transport immigrating refugees from Europe.

The common areas, though modest in size, were clean and comfortable. We ate our meals with pleasant American seamen in a dining room that accommodated everyone on board at one seating.

The deck area was large, with many chairs and chaise lounges. My parents and I shared a comfortable cabin with bunk beds. We settled in, expecting a pleasant and relatively short voyage. The captain enjoyed his nightly liquid refreshments that increased in quantity as the days passed. There were several young, single women on board, and we heard the captain every night as he banged on their doors.

The Mediterranean was calm as we set sail from Genoa. Our US destination had not been disclosed, and the crew was not forthcoming during the early days of the trip. The calm weather changed after a day or two. Rain and heavy winds prevailed, and the ship, devoid of its usual weight of cargo, heaved back and forth. My parents and I had never been out on the ocean, and we were frightened, but the worst was yet to come. The rain stopped, and the wind died down, but the ship was still. It couldn't move, because the propeller had broken.

The captain announced that help was on the way and that the propeller would soon be repaired. When help did not materialize, my parents were sure we'd have to abandon ship. Resigned to losing most of their very few belongings, they packed their essentials in a small bag. Then the wind again intensified, and we were tossed about a very turbulent Mediterranean. Unbeknownst to us, the crew had been working to repair the propeller for a day and a night. They finally succeeded, and again we were on our way.

The ship took a southern route. We ultimately found ourselves in the Caribbean, with days of continuous sunshine, blue skies, and calm waters. It had been years since the three of us had experienced such peace and unstructured, tension-free living. The food was good and plentiful, and the crew generally left us alone. All three of us spent much of each day on deck, relaxing in the sunshine. It was delightful.

My mother never traveled without a project. She had brought her knitting and diligently worked to finish a navy blue suit with a blue-and-white-striped sweater for herself, a red cardigan for me, and a beige pullover for my father. She completed all three by the time we reached America.

Early one afternoon, I left my parents on deck and headed for our cabin, where I lay down to take a nap. I must have fallen asleep immediately. My next memory is that of my mother vigorously shaking me and yelling, "Jutka, Jutka, wake up." I opened my eyes and realized the sun had set. My parents told me it was late evening and that I had slept for hours. They forced me to drink several glasses of water, and it took me just a few minutes to become fully alert. My father explained that I was dehydrated because I had been in the sun too long. They told me I had sunstroke. I had recovered by the next morning, except for the painful sunburn on my face, neck, and arms. We were all more careful from then on.

I was the only child on board, and the crew tried to be attentive. One morning an officer on deck approached me with a Hershey bar and urged me to consume it on the spot. In my halting English I explained that I hoped to share it with my father, who was more of a chocolate lover than I was. The officer was very persuasive, and I unwrapped the candy bar. Having spent almost two years in Switzerland, by that time I appreciated high-quality chocolate. The Hershey bar was not that. I took a bite and gagged—it was the most awful candy I had ever tasted. The ship's officer appeared very disappointed, and I made a rapid exit. To this day, I still don't like Hershey bars.

The 12 passengers on board were all engrossed in their own problems, and there was minimal intermingling. However, one question dominated all discussions: Where in the US would we dock? The crew either did not know or were not supposed to tell us. We had been at sea for over two weeks when we learned that our ship was headed for Gulfport, Mississippi. None of us had heard of Mississippi, and as for Gulfport? Where or what was that? No more information was available, not even how much longer we'd be at sea. A few days went by with no further news.

Then, suddenly, the captain announced our ETA, five days ahead. We docked in Gulfport five days later, on November 16, 1946, 22 days after embarking from Genoa.

Disembarking in Gulfport was tedious. We had two large suitcases and several smaller ones. My parents had purchased only necessities in Switzerland—they had no money to buy much. Nevertheless, our suitcases were filled with shoes that fit, coats that kept us warm, some new underwear, and books. Identification tags were mandated, and 50 or more pieces of tagged luggage were assembled on the gangway.

I was fascinated as I read the tags. A confused old Jewish refugee was headed for Latin America to join her rich children.

A single, elderly German-speaking man attended to her constantly during the journey. He told me his name was Jo Bejamiex, indicating that France was his original home. I observed him as he hauled his luggage to the gangway, and when he was out of sight, carefully inspected the luggage tags. The name on the tags was not Jo Bejamiex. I ran to tell my father. After examining the tags, my father took me aside and very quietly noted that the man's name was German and he was heading for Argentina. Later, I asked why a man would lie about his name. My father explained that he was most likely an escaping Nazi. We now know there were many such escapees.

Zoltan and Margaret had arranged train tickets for us from Gulfport to Washington, DC, but our departure time was later in the day. The ship line took our luggage to the railroad station, and we looked around for someplace to get a snack while we waited to board the train.

There were groups of American young women in the streets. My mother admired everything about them: their height, their hairstyles, their clothes, and their ever-present smiles. She was particularly impressed by their beautiful legs and the sheer nylon stockings they all wore. We continued to walk until we found a nearby coffee shop and sat down.

The waitress brought us menus. My father's mastery of the language surpassed my mother's and mine. Even so, he was not fluent in English and had never seen an English language menu. My European parents ordered bread, butter, and cheese. The waitress was puzzled and repeatedly asked, "You mean a cheese sandwich?" My father replied, "No. We want bread, butter, and cheese." The waitress spoke very slowly and smiled all the time. After minutes of frustration, she went to the kitchen and brought us what we had ordered. We devoured it all. I was amazed that we were able to order anything we wanted and even more surprised that all the menu items were available and affordable. It was a new experience.

We needed to use the restroom and were directed to the back of the building. There, in front of us were four clearly marked bathrooms. "Men, white. Women, white. Men, colored. Women, colored." My mother blanched. My father couldn't believe what he saw. After Nazi atrocities in Hungary and the Bergen-Belsen concentration camp, here was blatant racial discrimination in America, in the land of the free. I had never met or seen colored people. I wasn't even sure who they were. As a matter of fact, based on personal experience, I had believed Jews to be the only persecuted minority. I did not understand why my parents were upset and insisted on an explanation right then. My father very patiently told me about colored people and about racial discrimination, pointing out that there is much discrimination in the world and not only against Jews. Later, on the train to Washington, he told me about slavery, the Civil War, and Lincoln's Emancipation Proclamation. It was a very educational train ride, but I continued to be surprised that groups other than Jews had also suffered from indignities.

Disenchanted with our experience in the coffee shop, we hurried to the railroad station. Our recent train rides, from Bergen-Belsen to Switzerland and Switzerland to Italy, had resulted in good outcomes. However, as we approached the train station in Gulfport, memories of our earlier trip from Budapest to Bergen-Belsen began to haunt me. I repeatedly asked my mother and father if they were sure the train was safe. How could they be sure that we were not going to another concentration camp? My parents' reassurance ultimately pacified me. We found comfortable seats, and our journey began.

The three of us were mesmerized by the scenery we passed. Hour after hour we looked at Southern farms and plantations with acres and acres of land that was mostly dormant in the November weather. Since Békés, my Havas grandparents' hometown, was a farming community, much of what we saw was familiar. However, there were types of trees we had never seen before, ones that were mostly bare. Most surprising was the prevalence of machinery: cars, buses, tractors, and combines.

The roads we passed in the South were mostly paved, and cars moved along them in an orderly fashion. We wondered how a country could have so many paved roads. And who owned all the automobiles? The farmers in Békés had mostly used oxen, and the wagons that brought them to town were horse-drawn. Businessmen in town generally walked to work, though some rode their bicycles. The motorcycle and sidecar that my Uncle Laci rode all over town was a rarity.

Our fellow train passengers were friendly. Many smiled and greeted us as they passed. There were no uniformed personnel on the train, no police, and no soldiers. We had never experienced anything like it. No one asked to see our identification documents, and no one seemed to care who we were or where we might be going.

The sun sets early in November, and I fell asleep shortly after sunset. Gulfport and Washington, DC, are about 1,000 miles apart, and it must have been at least a two-day trip. I took several long naps and awoke to being shaken by my mother. "Jutka, Jutka, we are almost in Washington," she said. The train came to a full stop a few minutes later. It was the middle of the night. We put on our coats, collected our belongings, and got off the train.

All three of us were skinny, bedraggled, exhausted, and confused as we looked around the train platform. Then we heard excited shouts in Hungarian, saying "Ot vannak. Ot vannak"—"There they are. There they are." Seconds later, we were engulfed in the warm embraces of Zoltan, Margaret, and Gordon. It was a heartwarming welcome.

Zoltan went to get his car, and we loaded our belongings into the trunk. My parents and I rode in the back seat. Half an hour later we arrived at 1825 N. Powhatan Street in Arlington, Virginia. Zoltan parked his car and we went inside. We couldn't believe our eyes. There were three large rooms on the main floor, a living room, a dining room, and a kitchen, as well as a half bath. Upstairs there were three bedrooms and another bathroom. We had never seen so much space for just one family.

Aunt Margaret had prepared a sumptuous meal, and my parents were very appreciative. I was sleepy and tired and soon went to bed. My cousin, Gordon, was my new roommate.

I must have slept late the following morning, because the household was buzzing with activity when I awoke. Gordon was not in the room. I quickly dressed and went downstairs to explore my new home.

My impressions of the night before were reinforced. Sunlight filtered in through all the windows, and I thought I was in a magic castle. I repeatedly walked around the first floor, taking in all the beauty and luxuries it offered. The kitchen contained a big refrigerator, big enough to accommodate several days' worth of groceries. There was a breakfront containing a second set of dishes and serving utensils in the dining room. There was a screened porch furnished with a sofa and comfortable chairs, and the entry hall had a coat closet. I had heard that everyone in America was rich, and my aunt and uncle's home confirmed it.

We spent several days acclimating, sightseeing, eating, sleeping, and meeting Zoltan and Margaret's friends. I enjoyed every minute and was surprised to learn that I had to go to school.

I was nine years old in 1946, but I had attended school irregularly since the middle of first grade. In Switzerland, from ages eight to nine, my education had been unconventional. I had learned to speak German at boarding school, and my tutor had taught me math and English. As a result, I felt confident that my education would proceed smoothly.

Zoltan and Margaret lived in Arlington, and my neighborhood school was in Falls Church.

Zoltan drove me to school the first day. The red brick schoolhouse, though smaller than I had expected, was solid and real. I was excited to attend a regular school for the first time in three years. But fear of failing suddenly overwhelmed me, and I wanted to stay in the car. Zoltan persuaded me to go inside, and he walked me to the principal's office, where he and I told her my story. I had been certain I could meet the challenge of fourth grade, but the principal was not as confident. "She doesn't speak English, and she has not attended school regularly for at least two years," the principal said. Her uncertainty surprised me, as she had not addressed me at all but spoken about me in the third person as if I were not present, making me very uncomfortable. Zoltan convinced her to let me try fourth grade. As a result of the principal's comments, I lost self-confidence and was no longer convinced that American schooling was going to work for me.

The principal led me to a fourth-grade class and introduced me as Judith Gondos without any additional comments. During recess some students heard my halting, accented English, and some asked where I had come from. I told them about two years in Switzerland, time in a concentration camp in Germany, and Hungary. Most of my classmates were disinterested, while some considered me a novelty. They surrounded me in groups but posed no further questions.

School had begun around 9:00 in the morning. I had no idea when it would end. I wore a burgundy-colored wool dress with a white lace collar and sash the first day. It was the same dress I had worn to Rosh Hashanah services in Bergen-Belsen. I was two years older now, and the dress was too tight. Nevertheless, I felt very stylish as we drove to school and was surprised how out of place I looked. The girls at school all wore pastel-colored cotton dresses that were the right size.

At noon, all the children picked up milk they had pre-ordered, took their lunch boxes off the shelf, and began to eat. I had not brought a lunch and had not pre-ordered milk. Consequently, I just sat at my desk and salivated at the delicious smells of tuna sandwiches and peanut butter sandwiches around me, and at the sight of potato chips and cookies classmates pulled from their lunch boxes. I told Aunt Margaret that evening, and she packed me a light lunch from then on.

The teacher was a permanent substitute. She provided neither instructional help nor extra privileges. She expected me to keep up with the class and, for the most part, I did. However, I wished someone would help me adjust to a new American school, and I badly wanted assistance in unfamiliar subjects. No one offered, and I did not know whom to ask. Although I had no desire to be singled out for anything, I wished for more guidance.

At first I was exempted from reading out loud, a part of the daily reading program. After a few weeks in class, I was called on to read and performed acceptably, and I became a regular class reader. My math skills were far ahead of fourth-grade level, and I performed up to expectations in all other subjects. There was one ongoing problem: I talked too much. The teacher repeatedly asked me to quiet down in class. My incessant talking was reflected in my first report card a few weeks after enrolling. I had an A in both spelling and math but a C in citizenship, because I talked too much.

My classmates were friendly during the school day. They included me in their activities in class and at recess, but none of them expressed much interest in me outside of class, and no one invited me to their homes to play.

We had a weekly lesson in religion. Mine was a public school, but the Commonwealth of Virginia permitted a nonschool employee to teach weekly about Christianity. We heard stories about Jesus and drew many pictures of him as well. At holiday time there was Christmas-related education, decorations, and carols. This bothered me a great deal, but I was embarrassed to tell my parents. I had heard about freedom of religion in the United States and had been told that public schools did not provide religious education. I thought I had been misinformed and elected not to give my parents a new cause for worry. So I quietly endured this affront and mouthed rather than vocalized many of the carol words.

The permanent teacher returned early in 1947, and the substitute was no longer needed. She objected to everything I did: the way I read, the way I wrote, and the way I solved math problems. She was far more critical of my incessant talking than the substitute had been. It's hard to believe that I was as objectionable as she thought I was.

Meanwhile my parents had their own share of problems. Zoltan was a general practitioner. He tried to involve my father by sharing medical problems from his own practice. My father found this interesting, but it was not his specialty. He made contact with the chairman of radiology at Georgetown University Medical School. The two had common interests, and the chairman invited my father to visit and observe. My father gratefully spent many weekly hours at Georgetown. However, observing radiology at Georgetown was not the road to practicing radiology. It became apparent to my father that he needed American updating in his medical specialty.

EMBARKING TOWARD A NEW LIFE

My parents and I had no money and no source of income in Virginia. Though my aunt and uncle were generous, my parents were embarrassed to ask for money. My mother, who spoke very little English, found a job sewing lampshades in a shop on DuPont Circle. She had never made lampshades but quickly learned and began to earn enough to cover snacks, occasional movies, and some basic necessities. The work was menial, but she derived tremendous satisfaction from her earnings.

Then a radiology fellowship became available at Boston City Hospital, and my father applied and was accepted. It was a two-year fellowship with a total stipend of $2,400. My father left for the fellowship during the early spring, and my mother and I followed a few weeks later. We went to Union Station and boarded a train. We were headed for Boston.

CHAPTER 10

New Horizons

Early spring in Boston was beautiful, with green grass and bright yellow forsythias everywhere. The weather was cooler than it had been in Washington but not by much. Housing was hard to find due to increased demand from returning soldiers. Higher educational institutions were overrun with students who sought GI benefits at universities. This was the environment we encountered when my mother and I arrived at the railroad station. Apuka met us and explained that we would set out on a housing expedition the following day.

My father must have been in touch with a Jewish social service agency, but he did not mention it. I believe they provided him with a list of available housing, all in Brookline, a Boston suburb. Brookline was chosen for two reasons. First, the school system there had an excellent reputation. Second, there was good public transportation to downtown, the location of Boston City Hospital.

Our search for housing began on schedule the following morning. By early afternoon we had seen nothing but furnished single rooms with shared bathrooms and no kitchens. Apparently, there was nothing else. Then we found a decent room with a large attached porch in a stately Victorian house on Park Street. Out of options, my parents decided to rent it. We had neither a refrigerator nor a stove, so we purchased a hot plate and had to shop daily for groceries. Fortunately there were good bakeries, delicatessens, and grocery stores in the neighborhood, and we had no problem eating properly.

My father was gone from early morning until late at night much of the time. He slept at the hospital when on call, and we saw very little of him. His two-year $2,400 stipend would have been stretched very thin, but my mother, now with experience sewing lampshades in Washington, confidently responded to a "help wanted" sign at a lamp store on Harvard Street in Brookline and was instantly hired. Her salary of $40 a week was modest even by 1947 standards. However, we had no car and few home furnishings, and had purchased only the most essential clothing. With this pared-down lifestyle, we were able to exist mostly on my mother's earnings and saved the bulk of my father's compensation.

My neighborhood school was S. S. Pierce, and my parents promptly enrolled me there to finish fourth grade. School was almost over for the summer by then, and I recall very little.

Summer vacation soon began. School would not start for two

and a half months, and my parents, my father in particular, worried about my isolation and lack of activities. I was not concerned at all, because I loved the freedom to do as I pleased. My father devoted much of his limited free time, in the evenings and on weekends, to teaching me Hebrew. He gave me many time-consuming assignments. I did them all, and my progress was impressive. I visited my mother at the lamp store every afternoon, made friends with a kid who lived below us, and enjoyed listening to the radio, becoming a devoted fan of "The Romance of Helen Trent," "Oxydol's Own Ma Perkins," and "The Breakfast Club with Don McNeill." My father, however, felt I needed more structure.

One afternoon he came home in the middle of one of my soap operas and told me to put on my shoes because we were going to the Jewish Community Center, the JCC, where there was a nice day camp. I had no choice in the matter, so I put on my shoes, and we walked the mile or so to the JCC. The camp was great. A bus took us regularly to swim in Houghton's Pond, a natural spring-fed pond in nearby Milton. There were also many fun activities at the JCC itself, including art, drama, and music. I loved it and announced after a day or two that I wanted to return the following summer. We never discussed funding or even how my father found out about the camp. I now assume a Jewish social service agency had recommended the day camp and, possibly, even covered the fees.

We lived on Park Street for about a year while I attended S. S. Pierce School. My fifth-grade teacher was nice. She recognized that I was an impoverished refugee. I was an outsider there, as I had been in Virginia. I had made friends with a girl in my class, and her parents tried to be cordial by inviting me to join them at the circus, frequent lunches, and play dates. The problem was the girl, not her parents. She was controlling, overbearing, and insulting. "Shut up. Be quiet. You're stupid. You don't know anything," she would repeatedly say. I finally recognized her faults and refused to respond to her invitations. She and her parents were puzzled, but I had had enough put-downs to last me a lifetime. And I was proud I had asserted myself.

Then a furnished two-room apartment with a kitchen but shared bath opened up on 30 Beals Street, close to my mother's place of employment. Incidentally, this was the same street on which John F. Kennedy was born. The rent was $20 a week, $5 more than we had paid on Park Street. Anyuka and Apuka decided it was worth the difference, and we moved there at the end of the school year. As another advantage, it was also much closer to the JCC than our prior home was.

That next summer at the JCC there was an audition for the part of Gretel in "Hansel and Gretel," the annual musical, and I got the part. I must have sung on key. There were daily rehearsals, and I was a camp VIP. I enjoyed it all.

Edward Devotion School was my school for sixth grade. The student body was highly motivated and academically successful, and, in terms of schoolwork, I had a good year there. However, I just did not fit in. Most of the students came from upper-middle-class homes with professional, high-income fathers and stylish mothers. My father, though professional, earned a very modest living, and we lived in a very simple apartment.

My mother was not stylish, and despite my success at the JCC, I was not outgoing.

The Brookline schools provided free music instruction with free instruments, and I decided to study violin. The year of violin lessons was very enjoyable, but I refused to practice, much to the teacher's dismay.

A classmate who lived in our neighborhood became my best friend. I was a frequent guest in her home, and we often went to the movies together on Saturday afternoons. She was a very sweet girl, and her family liked me. Her mother occasionally visited mine at her workplace, and they were friendly as well. My winter coat was threadbare and not warm enough. I was certainly aware of this, but I didn't realize that others noticed. My friend and her older sister had gotten new coats. The sister's old coat was in good condition, and her mother offered it to me. After a certain amount of prodding, I accepted the coat, instinctively aware my mother would disapprove. Carrying my worn-out garment, I wore the "new" coat home. My mother immediately noticed, and I explained that no one at my friend's house could wear it. Mother was adamant, exclaiming that we did not accept clothing donations, and she instructed me to return the coat. Greatly embarrassed, I did so. To her credit, my friend's mother understood and told me the coat would be there for me any time I wanted to wear it, especially if I was going somewhere special. I thanked her, though I never wore it.

My father's fellowship ended in the spring of 1949, so he had to find a job. This was not easy. He had passed the Virginia

State Medical Board exams but was not yet board-certified in radiology. His mastery of the professional aspects of the English language was perfect, but his conversational English left a great deal to be desired.

In April of 1949 my father returned to Washington, DC, where he was very busy job-hunting, and there was very little communication between us. At the end of the school year my mother and I joined him. Father met us at the railroad station on crutches. Unknown to my mother and me, he had undergone a surgical meniscus repair. We were also surprised to hear that he had accepted two jobs and had arranged for the purchase of radiology equipment to begin a radiology private practice.

My parents were fiercely proud and independent, and I had previously assumed they refused financial assistance. This philosophy apparently had changed. I learned that a Jewish social service agency had covered my father's knee surgery expenses, along with the cost of our rooms at the Hotel 1440. As far as I know, that was only the second time he had accepted charitable help, the first time being for my day camp fees in Brookline.

We accepted help one other time, and that help made everything else possible. It came crucially at the very end of our naturalization process in 1951. I was really looking forward to becoming an American citizen, mostly because I wanted to be like everyone else. Reaching this milestone meant something entirely different to my parents: It meant our family's livelihood. My father needed US citizenship to be eligible for certification by the American Board of Radiology, an essential credential for a practicing radiologist. Additionally, they were anxious to be able to vote in elections, a right the Nazi-dominated Hungarian government had denied them.

The citizenship swearing-in ceremony was scheduled during business hours in Upper Marlboro, Maryland, the Prince George's County seat. Just minutes before the ceremony, the court clerk noticed an undocumented gap in my parents' American biographies and brought it to the presiding judge's attention. Consequently the judge refused to grant my parents citizenship unless a live witness could vouch for the time period in question.

In desperation they telephoned Sadie, a neighbor and friend. She had known my parents for over two years and, fortunately, was at home when they called. They implored her to rush to Upper Marlboro to testify on their behalf. Sadie found a babysitter, took a cab, and was at the courthouse within an hour, well before the end of the court session. Had she not gotten there in time, the swearing-in would have been postponed, perhaps for several months. Greatly impressed with the swift resolution of the problem, the judge expressed admiration for an immigrant physician who was providing dedicated service to the Defense Department, working as a radiologist at the Army Dispensary in the Pentagon. My father appreciated the compliment. For Sadie, the costs of a babysitter and cab fare were significant. Her husband was a PhD candidate, in school on the GI Bill. My parents paid her back swiftly and gratefully. After all the excitement, Ilona and Bela proudly left the courthouse that day as American citizens.

As a minor child of new citizens, I was automatically granted American citizenship and was included on my mother's document.

I had to wait until dinner that evening to hear the news because my parents had not permitted me to miss school on the big day. Disappointed not to have attended the ceremony and very independent by nature, I emphatically declared the intention to secure my own citizenship papers. My parents voiced no objections but indicated they had no time to get involved.

As in all bureaucracies, learning how to proceed was not easy. Everyone in Washington had the same response: No duplicate naturalization certificates could be issued, meaning that I could not get an independent naturalization certificate. I was undeterred and persisted with daily phone calls, often repeatedly, to the same obstinate bureaucrats. I was 15 years old at the time. A woman in the Department of Immigration and Naturalization seemed sympathetic and must have grown tired of my frequent phone calls. She finally agreed to work on issuing a document solely in my name. We made an appointment, and she instructed me to bring a passport-size photo and my Hungarian birth certificate. I did as instructed. The woman administered the citizenship oath, and, as my parents had done a few months earlier, I left her office as a proud American citizen in the spring of 1952.

My father's two part-time jobs as a radiologist at the Army Dispensary at the Pentagon and at the Group Health Association both provided steady income. His secondhand radiology equipment was purchased with a loan from an American physicians group established to help refugees. They did not expect repayment of the loan. Nevertheless, my parents repaid the funds in a few years. The two jobs and private practice involved a 60-plus hour workweek.

Once back in Washington, DC, my mother wanted to continue doing her share. She visited many furniture stores and decorating shops in the hope of finding a job. Lacking American credentials and unwilling to serve as an apprentice, she was unsuccessful. Discouraged, she finally offered her services to Bela, who gratefully accepted. He trained her as an X-ray technician. In the office she was also the receptionist, secretary, and bookkeeper. After a few weeks she concluded that the weekly cleaning woman was not earning her wages, and my mother became the cleaning crew as well. Although their income soon became healthy, the workload was almost unbearable for both of my parents.

There was a housing shortage in Washington too. After first spending several weeks in a residential hotel, my parents later found a two-bedroom apartment in the newly built Queenstown apartment complex in nearby Mt. Rainier, Maryland, in Prince George's County. There were many veterans there, some beginning their education on the GI Bill. Others were newcomers to Washington and government service.

Due to this influx of new residents, the phone companies could not keep up with demand for new telephone service in the metropolitan area. When we moved into our Queenstown apartment building, no resident had a telephone. My father, trying to build his radiology practice, was severely challenged as he tried to cope without a residential phone.

The situation also challenged Uncle Zoltan, who was trying to help my father. Zoltan referred many patients from his general practice in Northern Virginia. Some of the procedures required advance planning or preparation, and Zoltan had no direct way to notify my father of those patients' needs. This meant that several evenings a week Zoltan drove from his home in Arlington to our apartment in Mt. Rainier—about 45 minutes each way—to inform my father of the demands of next day's referrals. He provided this help cheerfully and willingly for several months until we finally received our phone. Fortunately, we were given priority because my father was a physician. Ours was the first phone in the building. I imagine Uncle Zoltan was at least as happy about that as we were.

We met many nice and interesting neighbors in Queenstown, and I enjoyed living there. Mt. Rainier Junior High was my new school. It was populated by some fellow residents of our apartment complex, as well as students from working-class neighborhoods. The teaching was not very good, and my parents were anxious to move, but the acute housing shortage continued to pose problems.

From our home in Mt. Rainier my father rode the bus to the Pentagon in Virginia where he worked, then to his private office at 1720 Connecticut Avenue NW in DC and then to Group Health, which was downtown. This was wasted time, which was something my father would not countenance because it diminished his productivity. A car became a necessity. Eventually my parents bought a new 1949 four-door black Chevy sedan. In Europe, very few people had cars, though with our urban lifestyle there, we hadn't needed one. Buying the car was a further financial strain in our early years in the US. My parents didn't know how to drive, so my father went to driving school to learn. My mother and I continued to use public transportation.

CHAPTER 11

Becoming American

One commute of my own brought a surprising realization of how different my life had been from that of my classmates. I was on a bus on the way to Sunday School on Mother's Day in 1950. From where we lived in Prince George's County at the time, I had to transfer and ride two buses in order to get to the Adas Israel synagogue at Connecticut Avenue and Porter Street NW in Washington, DC. I took the same bus every Sunday and most of the time rode with the same people on their way to church. It was a motley crew, all women of various ages and, judging by their dress, representing a broad spectrum of socioeconomic levels. We passengers developed a certain camaraderie over a period of weeks and worried when a regular was not on the bus.

All of the usual crowd was onboard that Mother's Day and happily discussed their plans for celebrations. Several of the passengers asked what I planned to do for my mother. In my family's experience in Hungary, Mother's Day had not been commercialized, so I had no plans. However, I was embarrassed to admit the truth and gave a fictionalized account of what we would do. As I continued to listen to my fellow passengers, I heard repeated references to grandmothers, all of whom seemed to be included in the day's festivities.

I was dumbfounded and finally blurted out, "What? You have grandmothers?" I couldn't believe it. Not only did I not have a grandmother, no one in our circle of Holocaust survivor friends had one. My parents and survivor friends had lost that entire generation of relatives in the Auschwitz gas chambers, their bodies unceremoniously burned in the crematoria.

That episode was a sadly revealing moment. I finally acknowledged what had happened to my family during the Holocaust. Other kids had grandparents, but I did not and would never again have the opportunity to benefit from the love, attention, and wisdom that only grandparents can offer.

A new chapter in our lives began when my parents bought a house on Donnybrook Drive in Chevy Chase, Maryland, shortly after New Year's Day in 1952. In addition to the fixed rate mortgage on the house, they had to take out a second mortgage, a small lien on the property at a higher interest rate. They rapidly paid off that lien. Although my grandparents had been homeowners in small towns, my parents had never before owned a home. They knew nothing about lawn care, fireplaces, or plumbing problems.

At home, my mother became a Jane-of-all-trades. She was an avid and expert gardener, an excellent cook, and a marvelous hostess. She had learned to sew with the Organization of Rehabilitation Training in Switzerland and made many of her own clothes and draperies. She also learned how to paint the house, inside and out. With a love of decorating, my mother soon attractively furnished the living areas. The neighbors, many professionals, provided an instant social network. There were no kids my age in my parent's group of friends, but I found friends in nearby neighborhoods.

Because of the move, I transferred to Leland Junior High School in Chevy Chase in the spring of 1952, near the end of my freshman year. The new school was an eye-opener. My math skills were less sophisticated than those of my fellow students, and the teacher offered after-school help for those of us who needed to brush up. There were about half a dozen kids at the first tutorial session. A student remarked about a very foul odor in the classroom, not designating a source of the odor. Grinning, the elderly teacher uttered a very distasteful, racially charged insult and asked, "Do you know what type of roses smell the worst?" Impressed with himself, the teacher answered his own question, "Negroes." He was convulsed with laughter as the class remained silent. There were no Negroes or other dark-skinned students in the class.

I was shocked. I stood up and exclaimed, "That's not funny. You've just insulted an entire group of people." I was trembling as I finished and expected to be thrown out of class, possibly expelled, and certainly to fail. None of my fears were realized, as I finished the class with an A. More importantly, that math teacher never again uttered a racially objectionable comment in my presence.

Our social studies teacher invited me to share some of my wartime experiences with the class. In my five and a half years in the US, no teacher had ever acknowledged my Holocaust background before, and no one else had ever invited me to share my background. Interestingly, I was not nervous as I spoke about Hungary, the Nazis, Bergen-Belsen, and Switzerland. At that time there were very few Jews in Bethesda and almost none at Leland Junior High. There were certainly no other Holocaust survivors. My talk lasted most of the afternoon. I suspect my classmates learned a great deal about many things of which they had been unaware.

I began 10th grade at Bethesda-Chevy Chase High School the following fall. I was now an American citizen and considered myself to be like everyone else. The problem was that I was not. The cultural gulf was still deep. I did not understand the things American kids did. I did not dress like them and did not even eat like them.

I had learned during the Holocaust that I could depend only on my parents. This sentiment prevailed in the United States, and I was still too dependent on them in high school. Their frame of reference was limited by their European experiences. I continued to be enveloped in their cocoon and lacked self-confidence. I sought their approval as I participated in activities such as Hebrew school, Sunday school, Shabbat services, and synagogue youth groups. I enjoyed these activities but avoided others in fear of disapproval. Clothing was another example. Teenage fashions, evident throughout my school, were appealing. My mother seemed unaware of adolescent desire to conform. She insisted that I wear only classic, high-quality clothing. So I generally looked frumpy, but I accepted it.

My parents gave me a weekly allowance to cover all incidental expenses, including lunches. School lunches seemed to be a waste of money. As with most institutional food, they were not particularly tasty, healthy, or satisfying. I gagged on peanut butter, a lunch staple for many of my friends, and I didn't particularly enjoy sandwiches. I preferred to bring my lunch. Generally I ate hard-boiled eggs, carrot sticks, celery, and an apple. My friends often went to a nearby Hot Shop to eat hamburgers and French fries. I had not developed a taste for such American lunches and preferred to save my money.

We ate European-style dinners at home. They consisted of complete, tasty, well-thought-out meals, including homemade soup and a Hungarian-style main course, such as stuffed peppers, stuffed cabbage, or veal. My mother always served vegetables and home-baked desserts. I assumed other families ate as we did. But eating dinner at friends' homes surprised me. Those meals consisted of one main course, such as spaghetti and meatballs, hamburgers, or fried chicken, all with only one side dish. We were not served appetizers or soups. Dessert, if served at all, came from a commercial bakery.

I was a good student and had some nice friends, but American high school culture remained foreign to me. My parents, of course, were not able to help.

I didn't understand the concept of school spirit, of cheering for your school team. What was football all about? What on earth were extracurricular activities? I didn't get it, no one explained it to me, and my parents did not know they should encourage such things. So I went through high school leaving at the final bell each day and never participated in any activities such as the school newspaper, yearbook, or student government. My class rank was high, yet I was not elected to the National Honor Society. I did not know then that membership depended on those extracurricular activities as well as class rank.

Over time I developed a group of friends at school, and I was less of an outsider than I had been. My high school friends were nonparticipants or unenthusiastic participants. Though we occasionally attended a pep rally or football game, I rarely understood what was happening. Sometimes we went to the movies or just went to the Hot Shop and spent many hours there discussing boys, popular singers, movie stars, and other matters important only to teenagers. I never ordered hamburgers and fries, though I sometimes ate orange sherbert topped with crushed cherries. Sitting in this typical American environment may have been my earliest experience in Americanization.

Adas Israel Synagogue, which we joined shortly after moving to the Washington area, was the focus of my high school social life.

BECOMING AMERICAN

In Hungary we celebrated Shabbat and other Jewish holidays, and our home was kosher, but most religious aspects of Judaism were unobserved. This was in sharp contrast to my father's Orthodox upbringing, where compliance with Jewish laws and customs was part of daily life. Our more limited religious observance in Budapest may have been influenced by the tendency of Hungarian Jews to assimilate, or by supplanting religious observance with Zionist activities to prepare for a future Jewish state. Bela became an active Zionist while a medical student and imbued me with the idea of going to Palestine. There was the itinerant rabbi who visited my boarding school in Switzerland, but I recall only his warmth and support, not his religious input, and religious school in Brookline left no memories. But later, activities at the Adas Israel Synagogue exposed me to positive and interesting aspects of Judaism, such as Jewish history, weekly Torah portion discussions, conversational Hebrew, and Israeli singing and dancing. This was my initial exposure to the beauty and significance of Jewish tradition and study, and I embraced it all. I joined Leaders Training Fellowship, a group that required Judaic study for membership. A small group of us who fulfilled the requirements usually met at someone's home on Saturday nights. United Synagogue Youth came later, and I was its first secretary in Washington, DC.

Many of my friends from Adas Israel enthusiastically attended Camp Ramah, a camp sponsored by the Conservative Movement of the United Synagogue, with close ties to the Jewish Theological Seminary. As much as I wanted to go, my parents could not afford to send me during our early years in Washington. In 1954, my junior year in high school, I learned that Ramah would accept

17-year-olds as part-time waiters and waitresses and part-time campers. This arrangement sufficiently reduced camp fees and enabled me to attend.

The summer at Camp Ramah in the Poconos was the highlight of my high school years. I swam in Lake Como, went on hikes in the mountains, helped build sets for the musical *Oklahoma*, and did more waitressing than I had anticipated. In spite of my heavy workload, I loved everything about Camp Ramah. The girls in my bunk became lifelong friends, and my experience in Jewish living changed my outlook. My Ramah summer was so memorable that I encouraged our children to spend their summers there. Diane, Dan, and Tom all went to Ramah, each for several summers. Jonathan chose to spend much of his summers at our lake house and attended Camp Herzl, where the time commitment was only three weeks.

My parents joined Congregation Ohr Kodesh, a synagogue much closer to home, and my Adas Israel ties gradually loosened.

During our early years in the DC area, my parents had seemed most comfortable with fellow Hungarians, mostly Hungarian Jewish physicians who had moved there after World War II. They quickly found one another and became a cohesive group, socially and professionally. It was comforting to socialize with people who were culturally similar. Such get-togethers, often in our home, provided an opportunity to share experiences and to speak Hungarian. My parents enjoyed it, but it did not enhance their assimilation into American culture. Those ties weakened as individuals in the group adjusted more successfully to American life.

I often came home with new attitudes or habits—which were generally unappreciated. My parents' word had always been the law, and it had never occurred to me to argue. My friends, on the other hand, frequently disputed the relevance of parental opinions, and I began to do the same. For example, I refused to honor their objection to a "no curfew night" for senior prom. After many hours of arguing, I solved the problem by spending the night at the home of my friend Anne. Anne's mother did not impose a curfew, and my parents never learned how late I stayed out. Listening to the radio was another instance. My mother and father used the radio only as a news source and could not understand why I listened to popular music. If I had to listen to music, why not Mozart or Beethoven? In their opinion, only classical music was worthwhile. They were never comfortable when a friend of mine they didn't know offered to drive me somewhere. Such disagreements diminished over time as my parents broadened their social circle and became more Americanized themselves. Of course, much of the discord between us was also typical of that between any teenager and her parents.

College became the prevalent topic at school, and I wanted to go away to study. I knew nothing about higher education in the US, and my parents knew even less. There was one college counselor at my high school for a class of about 550, so advice was not readily available.

George Washington University, located in nearby Washington, DC, was my parents' college choice for me. They offered me a car so I could live at home while attending GW. This was a tempting offer and a luxury, but I really felt the need to go away.

Once my father realized local colleges were not on my list, he encouraged me to attend a New England women's college. So I applied to Pembroke College, the women's section of Brown University.

Brown required a personal recommendation, and I had no idea how to proceed. One of our neighbors was a prominent government official, and, without asking permission, I used his name as a reference. My parents learned about this after the fact and insisted that I immediately call him to seek permission. Unfortunately, the neighbor had already received the recommendation form the previous day, so all I could do was apologize. He was very gracious and must have written me a glowing recommendation. Brown accepted me but declined to offer me a scholarship, which made the cost prohibitive.

A friend suggested the University of Michigan. I applied, was accepted, and planned to attend as an out-of-state student. Michigan did not offer me a scholarship either, but it was affordable: Tuition was $225 a semester, and the dorm fees were $1,100.

After graduating from high school I needed a summer job. With some help, I passed the Civil Service typing test and spent two months as a typist at the Pentagon in an office that processed passports for military dependents. The work was dull, and the permanent staff took advantage of summer student employees. A military officer headed the office. We saw him only briefly when he came in to sign the day's correspondence. The job did pay me well. My after-tax earnings that summer covered personal, out-of-pocket expenses for the first three semesters at Michigan. My first semester at Michigan began in September 1955.

Full of excitement and some trepidation, I boarded my first flight to Ann Arbor in September 1955. I had no reservations about the new phase of my life because my professional goals were clear: I was going to be a pediatrician. To achieve them I had to finish a premed undergraduate program, medical school, and a pediatric residency. Unlike me, some friends and acquaintances were not ashamed to admit that finding a husband was their major college goal. As comfortable as I was with my academic and professional plans, I had misgivings about living in a dormitory and feared not fitting in. I also wondered whether or not a heavy academic load and an active social life could coexist.

CHAPTER 12

College Years

My freshman year began with a heavy academic load and challenges I had not anticipated. Reba, a close high school friend, was my roommate. She and I were both goal-oriented and hardworking. Reba was a steady, comforting influence.

For the first time in my life, I began to think independently about myself and my goals. What did I really want to do with my life? Did I really want to go to medical school? Would the practice of medicine preclude raising a family? I had many questions but few answers. The girls on my floor were enrolled in a variety of programs: social work, nursing, English, premed, political science, and many more. These all sounded fascinating, and I wished I could study them all. Many also had boyfriends or were actively dating. Perhaps an academic and social life were not mutually exclusive.

The University of Michigan is a large institution, staffed by world-class faculty. Many faculty members, engaged in research, public service, and consulting, had light teaching commitments. But others took on substantial teaching loads, and some were memorable pedagogues. Noted professors were in high demand. Much to my disappointment, I never reached the top of a waiting list for a Shakespeare class, for example.

Late one Friday evening during my freshman year, after a marathon discussion about the world's problems with my dormmates at Michigan, we were all headed for bed. One of the girls remarked that tomorrow, a Saturday, would finally give her the opportunity to sleep in. Several others chimed in about the pleasures of sleeping in. I was puzzled but tried to keep my mouth shut. After a few seconds, I just couldn't help myself and asked, "Where do you usually sleep? Outdoors?" No one responded, probably because it was late and they were tired, or they thought I was making a bad joke. Reba, my thoughtful roommate, explained the phrase to me once we were back in our room. I've always been an early riser, and even as a college freshman I never did sleep in.

This was but one of my many linguistic blunders. I may have been technically fluent in English by then, but mastery of colloquial English and idioms was more difficult than learning the basic language. The girls in my dorm represented a broad spectrum of socioeconomic levels, many geographic regions, and a wide variety of interests. Many spoke formal, correct English, but some did not. I had attended American schools for nine years, but, like my parents, I did not use profanity. Many of the girls in my dormitory used four-letter words, to which I was unaccustomed. Reba and my other high school friends had a less colorful vocabulary than my dormmates.

Dressing presented another problem, just as it had in high school. I was a bona fide teenager when I started college, but I was still torn between my parents' European customs and what I observed my friends and classmates wearing. To my parents' thinking, "good clothes" were the ones that were the newest or most expensive and worn for social occasions, whether for dinner or visiting friends. My mother wore high heels, stockings, a fashionable suit or dress, and a hat (until the 1960s or so) even to backyard barbeques or morning coffee. My father wore older clothes for going to work at the hospital, but neither of my parents owned anything that could be called "casual" clothing. My mother still bought me high-quality, unstylish clothes.

Things were no better at U-M. The girls in my dorm all differed from one another, but there was one common denominator: They all had the right clothes. They wore lovely skirts and sweaters, many of them cashmere, to class. My wool skirts and blouses had been in the closet as long ago as sixth grade. The lesson I learned from my parents was to wear my good clothes when going on a date. Old clothes were for wearing to class. I had no appropriate clothes to wear day in and day out. No one explained to me that I was as likely to meet important people in class as I was to meet them elsewhere.

Outgrowing old habits was a slow process, partly because everything at Michigan was new and there was much to learn. I also felt constrained by my family's limited financial resources as "New Americans." My parents worked long and hard hours and provided everything I wanted, and I was very reluctant to ask for more. I had earned good wages as a Pentagon typist and was able to cover my out-of-pocket spending needs. But I was a very frugal freshman. In order to economize, I usually skipped Sunday night pizza outings, claiming either a dislike of pizza or too much homework.

On my very first Sunday in Ann Arbor, the promise of a free brunch propelled me and some new friends to our local Hillel, the international Jewish organization for campus life. It was a beautiful early fall day, and we agreed to dress in our preppiest clothes: Bermuda shorts and knee socks. (My mother had taken me shopping just before I left for Ann Arbor and, at my request, outfitted me with some basic preppy clothes.) Enjoying a beautiful walk in new surroundings, about eight of us looked forward to a good meal that perfectly fit my price range.

There were dozens of new students at Hillel that morning, and I was delighted to meet so many, particularly of the opposite sex. A very pleasant, smiling, impeccably dressed guy came over to introduce himself. He seemed older and more self-assured than the others. We chatted for a few minutes and then we were separated by the crowd. His name did not register with me. An hour or so later, he found me again and offered me a ride back home. It was too beautiful a day not to walk, and I declined his offer.

A few days later, someone named Dave Jacobs called. I had no idea who he was and quickly consulted my roommate, Reba. She remembered him from our brunch at Hillel as "that medical student with the convertible." Dave asked if I'd like to have dinner and a study date the following day. Inclined to refuse, I placed my hand over the receiver and consulted Reba. She emphatically mouthed a negative response. "But he's offering dinner," I said. With this information, she replied without hesitation, "Then go." And I did.

Like me, I learned, Dave was an only child. He lamented that his father had not lived long enough to learn of his acceptance to medical school. Dave was a senior at U-M Medical School and undecided about his specialty in the future. He was 23 years old when we met in 1955—five years my senior. It was his seventh year in Ann Arbor. As he assured me, "The place will grow on you."

Enthusiastically, I returned to the dorm that evening, ready to tell everyone what a nice time I'd had. My date with Dave—more specifically, dating a senior medical student with a convertible—impressed my dormmates. Apparently, Dave had also enjoyed the evening, because he called again the following day and frequently thereafter.

Freshman experiences at U-M resembled my time at Bethesda-Chevy Chase High School. There were plenty of opportunities for activities in Ann Arbor, but as in high school, I had no idea how to become involved, and I did not know whom to ask. As freshman year drew to a close, I was no more acclimated to America than I had been at the beginning of the year.

The University of Michigan is a huge institution, with over 20,000 students in 1955 and academic programs as diverse as medicine, teaching, and engineering. There were sorority and fraternity houses, special purpose residential houses, and dozens of organizations. Everyone with an interest could be accommodated, but there were some who sought no affiliation. The unaffiliated—and this group included me—were regarded as a subgroup, the GDIs (God Damn Independents). In other words, my unaffiliated friends and I occupied our own place in the dorm.

Vestiges of my foreign background persisted. As a small child in Hungary, antisemitism, Nazism, and World War II had prevented me from living the life of a normal child. Bergen-Belsen and then boarding school in Switzerland had also excluded me from the mainstream. I had been an outsider, and I did not know how to get inside or how to assert myself.

Social interaction was also culturally challenging for my family. "Calling," or spontaneous visiting, was a European custom. My parents enjoyed "dropping in" on friends. "Whom should we visit today?" was a common Sunday morning question. They telephoned a designated friend and, assuming they received a welcoming response, visited on Sunday afternoon. Occasionally, they dropped in unannounced. I assumed this was the appropriate way to socialize. We all learned much later that an invitation was a prerequisite for visiting.

My sophomore year at U-M was unsettling. I had enrolled at Michigan as a premed student, planning to become a pediatrician, but by my sophomore year I had lost interest in a medical career. Perhaps Dave occupied more time than my studies did.

I had abandoned plans for medical school, but I had not yet found a new path and learned just before school started that I'd have a new roommate. Being uncomfortable with the whole environment, I began to think of transferring to GW.

Reba and I had planned to room together in my sophomore year, but she married Victor, her longtime boyfriend, late in the summer of 1956 and did not return to Michigan. I liked Sue, the roommate I was assigned at the last minute, but I objected to her study habits. Typically, she did not read her textbook or notes until the night before an exam. She then studied all night and generally earned test scores over 95%. Sue, who earned a PhD in biochemistry, became one of my dearest friends. Her family in Detroit was working-class, and they all used language I had previously considered unacceptable. She and her family helped augment my modest and proper vocabulary. They exposed me to a previously unfamiliar lifestyle and served to hasten my Americanization.

CHAPTER 13

Family Life

It was toward the end of my freshman year that Dave's mother first invited me to dinner, and I guess I passed the test. Returning the favor, Dave came with me to Chevy Chase, Maryland, in June of 1956, and my parents liked him as well. We continued to date, and in March 1957, during my sophomore year and near the end of Dave's internship, we became engaged. Our August marriage was during Dave's first year of residency in pathology and my junior year as an undergraduate.

Marriage and a medical career seemed mutually exclusive, and I had chosen marriage. However, I was committed to finishing college. I transferred to the School of Education at U-M and attended classes until the day Diane was born. Much to my disappointment, the curriculum was not as intellectually stimulating as the liberal arts classes I had previously taken, such as history, philosophy, English, and French literature. Yet, surprisingly, a history of education course provided valuable insight. I learned that in the past, children had been regarded as miniature adults. Childhood, as such, had not yet been "discovered." I wondered how this concept could be applied to raising children during the Holocaust and my parents' own child-raising philosophies.

Our daughter Diane was born in 1958, a semester before I had finished college. And then the Army claimed Dave's services for the next two years. We went first to Fort Chaffee, Arkansas, and then to Fort Riley, Kansas. In Arkansas two courses by mail gave me an academic push forward, and Kansas State University enabled me to finish my undergraduate requirements and earn a BA degree from U-M. I had developed an interest in economics, and I was able to learn more at Kansas State as a graduate student. While we lived in Manhattan, Kansas, a Sheltie named Bo joined our family. Another bonus was being near Kansas City, where we spent some very pleasant weekends.

Dave's Army obligations ended after two years of military service and he then resumed his residency in Ann Arbor. Our son Dan was born there in 1961. While in Ann Arbor, I enrolled in more graduate-level economics courses. We were now a family of five: Dave and I, two children, and a dog.

Our expanded family next moved to Chicago, where Dave had been accepted into a blood banking/hematology fellowship. It was an unpleasant year, economically and socially: $200 a month rent was a financial strain, and we hardly knew anyone in the city. After the fellowship ended, we were ready to make a permanent move.

The decision about where to go next depended on the entire family's needs. Dave required a professional challenge. I insisted on a city large enough to support a university, a symphony, good art museums, fine schools, and a sizable Jewish community. These criteria ruled out several job offers. I had loved Kansas City when Dave was in the Army and was pleased when he accepted a position at Menorah Hospital there. We moved into a rental home on 92nd Street in Overland Park in 1963.

Menorah had an excellent medical staff, but the job was not a good fit. Dave moved on after two years and in 1965 became director of laboratories at Providence Hospital in Kansas City, Kansas. That institution later became Providence-St. Margaret Health Center. It was a Catholic hospital. The nuns there were appreciative, accommodating, and respectful. David's primary professional interest and forte was surgical pathology, but he also vastly expanded and automated the lab there. Dave worked at Providence for the next three decades.

When our son Tom was born in 1964, the rental house proved to be too small for our growing family, and we started house hunting. We had price constraints, required good public schools, wanted children in the neighborhood, and had to be reasonably close to Providence Hospital.

A very nice but unspectacular house on Overhill Road in Mission Hills filled our needs, and we purchased it on its first day on the market. Home values in Mission Hills in 1965 were divided into two categories: estate-sized homes in old Mission Hills, north of 63rd Street, and family-sized homes to the south. Our new home was well south of 63rd Street.

We moved in late spring of 1965, excited to start this new phase of our lives. Surprisingly, the children in the neighborhood paid no attention to our kids, and the adults ignored us as well. A neighbor told us she had received a letter from the realtor introducing the Jacobs family—an unusual communication. It didn't take long to understand what was happening: We were the first Jewish family on the block. Our original abstract of title contained a restrictive covenant intended to keep African Americans out of the development. Although the restrictive covenant contained nothing about Jews, we began to feel that some neighbors preferred to exclude Jews as well.

In 1948, the US Supreme Court struck down the enforceability of restrictive covenants that limited property sales to Caucasians. Aware of this ruling but fairly new to Kansas City, we were unconcerned with this issue. After moving to Overhill Road we discovered there were some who remained concerned. While these covenants were no longer enforceable, they would not become illegal until 1968. However, some of those who had originally agreed to them may still have been committed to the original intent. Our family was confronted with the ugly fact that as Jews, we were unwelcome by many of our new neighbors. For me, a Holocaust survivor, the implications were devastating.

Not long after our move, a nearby Jewish-owned home was sold to a Black family. The father, a physician, had been a high-level federal government official in Washington, DC, and had come to Kansas City, as a physician, to assume a new position.

Our neighbors gave them a welcome similar to the one they had given to us. A smiling bigot on our street told me she would gladly have bought the house from the Jewish family to keep out the new "unwanted" family. She was convinced property values would soon decline. Left unsaid but implicit in her comment was that now there were two "unwanted" families on the block bringing down the neighborhood. Chatting at the foot of the driveway, I mentioned to the woman that we certainly lived "in the slums of Mission Hills." My comments were unwelcome, to say the least. Sadly, the Black family did not stay long in our neighborhood.

Once a year or two had passed, children from the opposite side of the street occasionally came to play at our house, but our kids rarely went to their homes. After engaging with those kids in the front yard one day, Tom, not yet three, walked into the kitchen and asked, "Mommy, are I a Jew snot?" After explaining to him that the insult was not a reflection on him but a reflection on the other boy, I called the boy's mother and shared what had happened. She expressed no regret and did not apologize. Her only comment was, "My husband will be so mad." I interpreted her comment as saying that her husband would be upset that I had acknowledged their prejudice.

I didn't think his first encounter with antisemitism left much of an impression on Tom, but apparently it did. He recently recalled the situation clearly, in great detail, after so many years. I do know that it immediately affected Dave and me.

A few more years passed after that incident on Overhill Road, and some neighbors began to express appreciation for our well-maintained yard. Several other Jewish families had purchased homes on our street by this time, and gradually the environment became friendlier.

Jonathan, our youngest, was born in 1968. I now had four children at home, along with a job as business manager to Dave's pathology group and a husband with insufficient time to shoulder many family responsibilities. We began to think more about what our children were learning about Judaism.

Dave and I concluded that providing our children with a strong Jewish education would enhance their Jewish identity, make them proud and knowledgeable Jews, and give them the strength and knowledge to deal with similar insults in the future, should they occur. Diane was enrolled at Prairie School, which was public, but all three of our sons began school at Hebrew Academy, now the Hyman Brand Hebrew Academy. All three later transferred to Pembroke Hill.

While sure of the schools I wanted them all to attend, I lacked schooling in American parenting. I was still a greenhorn. For example, I had no idea about the custom of attending children's athletic events. Dan, our oldest son, had been an enthusiastic soccer player since elementary school. I made sure he had transportation to and from his games, and occasionally I stayed to watch. My time was more limited when he reached high school, and I missed most of his varsity soccer games. Tom, our second son, was also a soccer player, and I missed most of his games as well. By the time our third son, Jonathan, reached high school and played American football, I finally understood and attended most of his football games.

As another aspect of our American Dream, we had some wonderful dogs. After our first dog, Bo, passed away some time in the late 1960s, there was Laddie, a large, beautiful collie. We loved him, although the neighbors were less fond. Loud and rambunctious, he was very intimidating, to the point that people got nervous when coming up to the house.

Unfortunately Laddie was not with us long; he only lived a few years. Our next dog was Perry, a pedigreed Shetland sheepdog, who ruled the roost. He was protective and noisy—characteristics that described the rest of us as well. Perry and the children learned to play basketball together in our driveway. Frankly, Perry was the most enthusiastic basketball player in the family. He was with us from 1974 until he died in 1989.

When Perry died of old age in 1989, Dave and I agreed to have no more pets. That agreement held for a time, but life happens. When Jonathan and Sherri married a few years later, it was soon apparent that Plato, Jonathan's Sheltie, was incompatible with Sugar, the original canine resident of their household. Contrary to our "no more dogs agreement," we gladly welcomed Plato into our home and thoroughly enjoyed his company for the better part of a decade.

Through much of the 1960s I had voluntarily helped Dave in his practice, mostly providing personal insight as I reviewed financial statements, contracts, and employee benefits. The practice grew exponentially, and I became its business manager around 1967. We incorporated as Pathologists Chartered in 1972. Along with the increase in surgical specimens and laboratory tests, there was more need for administrative oversight and general management, and I assumed more responsibilities. I worked from my home office at what began as a part-time job. However, it rapidly developed into a very labor-intensive endeavor. We expanded the deferred compensation plan, and I began to study investing.

I believe Jewish people in general have a deep-seated sense that education is the one thing that nobody can take from you. They can take your property, your possessions, your prosperity—even the food from your mouth and clothes on your back. Education, your personal knowledge, is the only thing that's yours alone and forever.

Family tradition, on both Dave's side and mine, bore that out through achievement and excellence. My paternal grandfather, Mor Goldman, was a college-trained teacher and, later, a principal. Three of his five children—my father, Bela, and his brothers, Sandor and Zoltan—were university educated. Several of my father's first cousins in Hungary were physicians, engineers, and teachers. Even my paternal grandmother's sister attended a school for the deaf in Budapest when few women were educated.

My father, as a radiologist, had to invest both time and effort to maintain his professional skills. He did so in Hungary before and during the war, in Switzerland immediately after the war and again when we moved to America. Later, as an academic radiologist, he read and studied incessantly and was a powerful role model for his grandchildren.

Dave's maternal grandparents came here from Eastern Europe with no formal education. They had eight children, five of whom became college-educated professionals.

Dave's mother, Rae Goldman Jacobs, graduated from the University of Illinois in 1914. At first she was a high school English teacher and later became a social worker. Then she worked as a juvenile court probation officer in Detroit until Dave was born. A smart, intellectual woman with very high academic standards, she often read to the children when they were little and encouraged them to read all they could on their own.

Dave and I never doubted that we should provide for our four children's educations as our families had done for us. They had lived modestly to pay for U-M, and Dave and I planned to follow their lead. We lived simply early in our marriage, as we tried to accumulate resources for future college tuitions. The children often lacked luxuries enjoyed by some of their friends, but they had reason to be optimistic about our financial support in college. Dave and I were pleased to have financed all of our children's educations and overwhelmingly proud when they thanked us.

Dave himself was a lifelong student and teacher and thus a strong role model for our family. He studied all medical literature relevant to patient care, not only pathology but all aspects of medicine. He read broadly in order to teach pathology residents, medical students, and medical technologists. Dave became the editor-in-chief and primary author of the *Laboratory Test*

Handbook, first published in 1980. Multiple editions followed, and it was the definitive reference for laboratory medicine in its time.

I have been academically motivated my entire life, and I strongly impressed upon the children the value of education and the importance of attending the best colleges that would accept them. Where education was concerned, I expected optimal outcomes (although of course my definition of optimal didn't always correspond with theirs). With rich family history and tradition behind them, each of our children found their own path to education.

Diane enrolled at Dave's and my alma mater, the University of Michigan, in the fall of 1976. She dropped out of school after her sophomore year and sold ladies' scarves and belts in Ann Arbor. She subsequently transferred to the University of Missouri–Kansas City (UMKC) and graduated in 1981 with a double major: a BA in communications and a BA in economics. Diane decided to pursue a career in journalism and attended Northwestern's Medill School of Journalism, graduating in the summer of 1982.

Her first job that same year was as a reporter and morning news anchor for a TV station in Jonesboro, Arkansas. After climbing the ladder for a few years, she got an on-camera job at the NBC affiliate in Dallas. She worked there for about two years before deciding to explore other career opportunities.

Diane spent two years as a legislative aide to a Texas state senator and, while working there, decided to go to law school. She attended Southern Methodist University Law School in Dallas and received her juris doctorate in 1993. Diane has had several interesting jobs. She began working at the Texas attorney general's office in the Civil Medicaid Fraud Division in 2002, where she has been an assistant attorney general and managing attorney, work she has greatly enjoyed. She retired in April 2023. Eli, Diane's son, now 21, is a senior chemical engineering student at the University of Kansas (KU).

Dan went to Stanford, where he not only majored in history but also fulfilled the science requirements to prepare for medical school. He graduated from Stanford in 1982 and began medical school at KU that fall. In 1984, Dan decided to spend a year abroad in Israel. Wanting to keep him interested in medicine, my father urged Dan to seek a preceptorship in radiology at Hadassah Hospital in Jerusalem, where Bela himself had done volunteer work several times. There Dan met his future wife, Cori, who was enrolled in the same program. Cori is now a board-certified ob-gyn.

In 1986, with his MD degree from KU in hand, Dan began a psychiatry residency at the University of Iowa in Iowa City. He enjoyed the program and the place but decided to seek a different specialty. After a year in internal medicine while Cori finished an ob-gyn residency at Johns Hopkins, Dan and Cori married in Baltimore in 1988. They returned to Kansas City the following year, and Dan began a three-year neurology residency at KU. Their children, Max and Annie, were both born in Kansas City, in 1989 and 1991. After a behavioral neurology fellowship and an academic position at Tufts University Medical School, Dan and his family moved to Orlando, Florida. They have lived and practiced medicine there for over two decades. Dan and Cori are now grandparents of Sammy.

Tom entered Duke University in the fall of 1982 as an engineering student. He realized within a few weeks that engineering was not a good fit and switched majors to graduate in 1986 with a BA in comparative studies. While an undergraduate, he spent a semester in Lima, Peru. Tom also developed an interest in forestry and was a US Forestry Service firefighter one summer during college.

Tom's experience in the Forest Service evolved into interest in the environment, leading to his MA in environmental management from Duke. He spent two years in the Peace Corps, serving first in Ecuador and then in Chile. In Ecuador he helped farmers manage their land, and he taught community development and agroforestry at the University of Chile School of Forestry in Santiago. After the Peace Corps, he earned an MS degree in sociology at Cornell. Tom currently is chief resiliency officer and director of environmental programs at the Mid America Regional Council, in Kansas City, primarily involved in climate change and other environmental issues. Tom married Barb Wishnow in 1994, and they are the parents of Forrest, now 19, a sophomore at Tulane. Though Tom and Barb are divorced, Barb remains an integral part of our family.

Jonathan had excelled in the sciences in high school and enrolled as an engineering student at Columbia. He soon decided against engineering and began taking premed courses in his sophomore year. Fulfilling the premed requirements in summer school took him to Rockhurst University for physics and Georgetown University for organic chemistry. Jonathan earned a BA in history from Columbia University in 1990. Mayo Medical

School was his first choice. He was awarded his MD at Mayo Medical School in 1995.

He then took a four-year residency in internal medicine and pediatrics at the Cleveland Clinic and finished in 1999. Jonathan has practiced internal medicine, first in Alabama and then in Overland Park, Kansas. He maintains credentials in pediatrics, but currently he mostly treats adults. In a volunteer capacity, Jonathan is the medical director of Care Beyond the Boulevard, a nonprofit organization that provides medical services to the homeless. Jonathan and Sherri, an artist and art and family therapist, were married in 2007. They have four children, Ariel, Avi, Ezra, and Rachel, and two grandchildren, Simcha and Tova.

I may have questioned my parenting skills when my children were growing up, wondering what I was doing wrong. But they have all developed into remarkable adults: amazing parents and highly ethical people who are productive, self-sufficient, and working to make the world a better place. I am very proud of them all.

As for myself, I returned to school in 1973—the same time my son Jonathan started kindergarten—as a student in the MBA program at the University of Missouri–Kansas City, with finance and investments as my primary interests.

In 1977, after completing my MBA, I hoped to become an economic researcher at Kansas City's Federal Reserve Bank. That goal seemed entirely realistic until I assessed it in greater detail. The cost-benefit analysis was shocking. I already paid taxes on my earnings but had not considered multiple other costs, primarily the wages of a full-time housekeeper. To my chagrin, it would cost me money—quite a bit of money—to work elsewhere. Disappointed but pragmatic, I agreed to stay on as business manager of Pathologists Chartered.

Still seeking more intellectual stimulation, in 1978 I enrolled at UMKC in a Higher Educational Administration PhD program with a finance concentration. The goal for my doctorate was to combine my earlier interest in education with expertise in finance. When finished, I hoped to teach colleges and universities to allocate and spend their funds effectively. It was again an incredibly hectic schedule for me, but as before, the family and Pathologists Chartered survived.

This time I was determined to pursue my career goal in higher educational finance, until reality once again changed those plans. My advisor informed me there were no such positions available locally and suggested I look elsewhere. We had no plans to move, so I stayed on as business manager of Pathologists Chartered. The job continued to be demanding, but gradually became interesting. New regulations increased my workload: Compliance with the Employee Retirement Income Security Act, for example, was expensive and time-consuming. We required frequent interpretation of the statutes and became much too dependent on legal services.

Becoming familiar with the Tax Equity and Fiscal Responsibility Act also expanded the scope of my responsibilities. They included hiring and overseeing a billing service, negotiating third-party contracts, and dealing with federal oversight. These were challenging activities and often satisfying. I became conversant in a new language—the language of medical business, and

I developed skills in finding and evaluating investment advisors, accountants, attorneys, billing agencies, and collection agencies.

The job continued to be a full-time position until Dave retired in 1994. The pathologists in the group found other jobs, locally and out of town. Winding down the corporation was more complicated than I had expected. Even with a diminished workload, it took about 18 months to wrap up corporate affairs. After almost 29 years, in 1996, I was finally finished.

CHAPTER 14

Other Remembrances

My family were landlubbers. My parents were enthusiastic swimmers but otherwise had no access to water sports. Boat ownership—sailboats or motorboats—was reserved for the Hungarian gentry. We were middle-class Jews, certainly not gentry. While I was growing up in Chevy Chase, Maryland, it never occurred to my parents to go out on anything other than a rowboat, a mentality I fully supported.

Dave was born in Detroit and lived there until he went to Ann Arbor to attend U-M. Michigan and nearby Canada are both dotted with lakes, big and small. Dave and his mother spent their summers in lakeside cottages, while Dave's father, Harry, worked in the men's clothing store he owned. Occasionally, Harry joined them for a weekend. As far as I know they never owned a boat, but they swam in the lakes and probably rowed a boat and went canoeing and kayaking.

Dave worked in high school and used his earnings to buy a used wooden canoe that he refurbished and refinished. He proudly dubbed it *Kon-Tiki*. While an undergraduate, he joined a canoe club and took *Kon-Tiki* on many trips throughout Michigan.

When we became engaged, Dave had a 10-foot wooden power boat, anchored in a nearby marina. There was at least one hole in the hull, and on the rare occasions we had time to use the boat, it was partly submerged. More often than not, we spent hours bailing water and then had no time to enjoy the boat or the water. Dave sold that boat by the time we were married.

Watercraft became much more a part of our lives after we moved to the Kansas City area. Dave decided to buy a sailboat, and with my characteristic sarcasm, I suggested that he shop at a local toy store. He did not follow my advice. Aware that only small, man-made lakes existed in the Kansas City area, Dave purchased a 12-foot Aquacat, a fiberglass catamaran that we sailed on Wyandotte Lake. At 400 acres, the lake was too small to challenge a real sailor, but it was very comfortable for me, although we soon mutually acknowledged my inadequacy as crew.

A Hobie 16, a somewhat larger and faster catamaran, followed the Aquacat. We lived on Overhill Road by then, and Dave joined a Lake Jacomo sailing club. There, with a 970-acre lake to work with, his sailing skills noticeably improved, and he began to participate in weekly races. One by one, all four of our children learned to sail, then to race, with their father. With or without our children, Dave kept on losing races. Having a Hobie

16, a larger but younger man's boat, had not enhanced his ability to win. He often lamented that in his mid-thirties he was the oldest guy in the club.

For Dave's next sailing adventure, he took on more water and took all of us along for the ride. The widest part of the Lake of the Ozarks extends for seven or eight miles south from Bagnell Dam. It's considered the best sailing area on the Lake. In 1980 we purchased a lakefront house there, just large enough for our family of six. We were two and a half miles from the dam. In later years, we had annual family get-togethers there. It was a wonderful setting for us, the children, and their friends. Dave enthusiastically continued to sail with the kids and taught them to water ski as well. Diane, Dan, Tom, and Jonathan became proficient at both.

The Hobie 16 came along with us, and we bought a power boat to complete the fleet. However, the Lake of the Ozarks proved too rough for a 16-foot Hobie, and we replaced it with an 18-foot Nacra catamaran. Dave and our children loved it. Our grandchildren Max and Annie learned to sail on the Nacra. The boat comfortably accommodated two sailors, even three on occasion. The boys learned to fly a hull and hike out. Undeterred when it turned over and they fell into the water, the kids righted the boat, jumped back on, and continued sailing. We often followed them in the speedboat, cameras in hand.

Even as the landlubber in the family, I became an enthusiastic boat owner. I loved cruising around the lake in the speedboat with or without a destination, visiting friends or going out to eat. I loved the feel of the wind in my face as we bounded across open water. However, I never quite experienced the euphoria of sailing. When there was no wind, sitting on a sailboat was extremely dull. Once the wind picked up and the boat took off, I was scared out of my wits.

Though the Nacra was frequently becalmed, Dave refused to add a motor, insisting that additional weight would slow it down. The rest of us were convinced he considered a motor to be an affront to his sailing ability. I vividly recall watching an embarrassed Dave sitting on the deck as Diane, holding a line, swam the boat home.

The Nacra required a crew of two. Ever adventurous, Dave wanted a boat he could sail single-handedly, so we bought the *Annie*, named for our only granddaughter at the time. It was a 21-foot Precision, a keel boat, big enough to have a galley and a head, although we never made use of either.

Dave was able to sail *Annie* alone when there were no children or friends available. Diane, Dan and Cori, Tom, and Jonathan and Sherri, as well as grandchildren Max, Annie, Ariel, Avi, Eli, Forrest, Rachel, and Ezra, all enjoyed the boat. The experience left a lasting impression. Sailing had become an integral part of our children's lives, as it had been a part of Dave's. Jonathan inherited the Nacra, which he subsequently gifted to a cousin in Alabama. Diane has owned a Sunfish sailboat for over three decades. Our granddaughter Annie will become its owner in the near future. Dan owned a Hobie 17 for a long time and sold it just a few years ago. Two fiberglass canoes still occupy his driveway. The Jacobs family's loyalty to the Hobie brand has not waned. Tom owns a Hobie kayak with sails.

The stairway down from the lake house to our boat dock was equivalent to about three stories, and it eventually became very difficult for Dave to manage the climb. We sold Annie around 2013 but kept the speedboat. It was in use until we sold the lake house in 2017.

Dave struggled with a plethora of medical problems that really began in the 1980s. A diagnosis of Crohn's disease led to two major surgeries. In 1991 he was diagnosed with multiple liver abscesses and later, AA amyloidosis, rectal cancer, and Waldenström macroglobulinemia, leading to consultations with physicians around Kansas City and the Mayo Clinic. All things considered, he was amazed to have lived so long.

Bad news continued into the 1990s. In 1991 Dave was diagnosed with liver abscesses in February and spent three weeks as an inpatient at the Mayo Clinic. After all that, on the first morning back home following Dave's return from Mayo, a neighbor pounded on the door to say our house was on fire. Weak and still receiving intravenous antibiotics, Dave picked up his IV stand, draped his coat over one shoulder, and we escaped outdoors.

The upper floor of our house was engulfed in flames a few minutes later, and the firefighters fought the fire for most of the day. By late afternoon the second story was gone, but the first floor remained mostly intact. Many of our belongings had not burned—including furniture, artwork, important papers, and photographs—and they were hauled to a storage facility. We thought a guard for the night might be useful, but the insurance company disagreed, deeming it an unnecessary expenditure. Exhausted, we went to sleep at our son and daughter-in-law's home.

Around 2:00 a.m. a neighbor called to tell us that the fire had reignited. Unfortunately this time, there was very little left of the house by the time we arrived.

The next few days were overwhelming as we talked with fire investigators, insurance adjusters, our attorney, architects, and contractors. No one was able to conclusively determine how or why the fire had begun, but over time we concluded that it must have been an electrical fire. Dave and I had two options: We could rebuild or sell the lot and buy another home. We selected the latter, and our search began.

By the time the house on Overhill Road burned down, we had become empty-nesters and had previously discussed downsizing. Now we were relieved of the decision of whether or not to move and could focus on where. Providence-St. Margaret's Health Center had relocated to western Wyandotte County, easily accessed by I-435, and by this time, that easy access was a priority for us.

We toured many houses in Johnson County and really liked a property on Wycklow. The house and lot were much too large—the house was about a third larger than our previous home, and the lot was double the size of our Mission Hills lot. The house on Wycklow was fully landscaped and contained a rock-surrounded swimming pool. Despite our idea of downsizing, we upsized instead. Dave and I now had gained space to pursue our interests without bothering each other. The size of the house and the swimming pool became magnets for our expanding family.

Dave remarked that the only way he would leave our home on Wycklow was in a wooden box.

That house was our home for 30 years, and it was a delightful place to live, even if it lacked the history and the nostalgia of our prior home. Our children had grown up in Mission Hills, our family marked many occasions on Overhill Road, and we had celebrated family events there with my parents and Dave's mother. Moving signified leaving behind a big slice of family history and transitioning to the next phase of our lives. We'd lost more than a piece of real estate as a result of that fire, and I continue to miss the white house on Overhill Road.

CHAPTER 15

The Past Recalled for Good

Part of our extended family, some of our family's lifelong friends, were Hungarian Jews, otherwise a heterogeneous group. They had all succeeded in their respective professions but desired to maintain ties to their origins. These families were part of childhood for all my children. In a sense, they replaced the family we had lost in the Holocaust.

Once in America the Holocaust was rarely discussed in our home and most likely in anyone else's. Survivor guilt understandably plagued my father in his post–World War II years. We avoided discussing the Holocaust while I lived with my parents, and I paid scant attention to the topic until the 1960s. By that time, I had a family and the perspective only time could provide.

The silence surrounding the Holocaust dramatically changed with television coverage of the Adolf Eichmann trial in 1961. Otto Adolf Eichmann, an Obersturmbannführer (lieutenant colonel) in Hitler's SS corps, was instrumental in organizing what the Nazis called the "Final Solution to the Jewish problem" and what we call "the Holocaust." In short, the extermination of the Jewish people. Eichmann was executed for his crimes, and most watched in horror, some in fascination, as facts of the evil perpetrated by Hitler and his henchmen were broadcast to millions of viewers around the world. The reaction was monumental, and the world was intent on learning more about Nazi atrocities.

Holocaust interest strengthened during the 1960s through not only the Eichmann trial but also the Six-Day War. June 5–10, 1967. Israel, threatened by a coalition of surrounding countries—led by Syria, Egypt, and Jordan—launched a preemptive assault. Israel achieved a decisive victory and gained control of the West Bank, Sinai, the Gaza strip, the Old City of Jerusalem, and the Golan Heights, and the map of the Mideast was redrawn. We had young children in the 1960s and wanted to provide them with Jewish identity and broad Jewish education. In addition to enrolling the children in Jewish day school, our family attended synagogue services, and all four children went to Jewish summer camps. Not only had our offspring developed strong Jewish identities, but Dave's and mine were strengthened as well. Still, I was not yet ready to revisit the horrors of the 1940s, and neither were my parents.

In the 1970s, Holocaust education became an integral part of many curricula. Diane and Dan, then Tom and Jonathan, all learned of Nazi atrocities at school. They wanted to know more. I always answered their questions but was reluctant to elaborate. There were many survivors in Kansas City better able to share their experiences than I was. The kids grew up, left the nest, and largely stopped asking questions.

In our new home in 1991, media outlets started asking for interviews. The first of these was the Fortunoff Video Archive for Holocaust Testimonies, which had originated as the Holocaust Survivors Film Project in 1979 in New Haven, Connecticut. In 1981, the Project's original collection of videotaped interviews with survivors and witnesses was donated to Yale University. A year later, the library opened the Video Archives for Holocaust Testimonies to the public. From that point on, the Fortunoff Archive has continued the work of recording, collecting, and preserving testimonies of those who experienced and survived the Holocaust. The archive currently holds over 4,400 interviews comprising over 12,000 hours of footage available to researchers, educators, and the general public.

As I do for all projects, I prepared well for their interview. It was my first experience assembling memories and observations about the Holocaust. Preparation, more than the actual interview, was an emotional experience. "How could God have allowed this to happen?" was a question that repeatedly ran through my mind. It was unsettling.

Not long after that experience, I was interviewed as part of the Spielberg Project. It, too, was emotionally draining. That collection of interviews grew out of Steven Spielberg's making of the 1993 film *Schindler's List*. The stories Spielberg gathered are housed at the University of Southern California and are part of what is now known as the USC Shoah Foundation. That foundation continues to gather not only Holocaust remembrances, but also testimony from survivors and witnesses to other attempts at genocide in places such as Rwanda, Guatemala, Cambodia, Myanmar, South Sudan, and Armenia. Though the scale of the Holocaust was unprecedented, the concept prevails.

Steven Spielberg ends the opening video on the Shoah Foundation's website by saying, "These survivors who are now educators, they can change the world." In my way, I continue to try to do this.

My parents had a storybook marriage. Their love and respect for each other, their willingness to work hard, and their resilience were an inspiration to the entire Jacobs family. Her now-adult grandchildren still speak lovingly about the adventures they had with "Washington Grandma." Her love of family and ability to promote family unity are legendary.

Ilona supported Bela in everything he undertook. She was his greatest fan and he, hers.

My mother was diagnosed with breast carcinoma in 1974, at 64 years of age. Her surgeon performed a radical mastectomy, and she was asymptomatic for eight years, during which she continued to live a very full and happy life. In 1982, a plethora of symptoms and untold number of diagnostic procedures led to a diagnosis of multiple metastases. She was repeatedly treated with radiation and chemotherapy. The two treatments delayed but did not stop further spreading of the disease, and the radiation and the chemotherapy had devastating side effects. She suffered, rarely complaining, during the final three years of her life. My mother died at age 75, on December 21, 1985, in Silver Spring, Maryland.

Bela Gondos was a highly productive radiologist, a loving husband, and an attentive father and grandfather. As he approached retirement, my mother feared possible inactivity and boredom. "What will he do?" she repeatedly asked. To stimulate interesting activities in the post-practice years, she bought him the 16-volume *Encyclopedia Judaica*, with annual supplements covering the Jewish people, Judaism, and Israel.

Retirement, along with the new reference materials, offered my father the opportunity to learn about various aspects of Jewish history in greater depth. At first he studied broadly, but over a two-year period he narrowed his interest to history of the Holocaust and then to the history of the Hungarian Holocaust. He shared his knowledge with many groups and became a Holocaust speaker. Books covered every horizontal surface of his home, including the floors. The living room was mostly an obstacle course, a testament to his interests and accomplishments. Studying about the Hungarian Holocaust consumed all of his time in retirement, just as radiology had done during his working years.

My father remained for 12 years in the house he had shared with my mother, where he continued to lead an interesting, satisfying, and productive life. He was blessed with relatively good health, an agile and inquisitive mind, good friends and neighbors, and sufficient resources to pay for anything he needed.

We began to worry about him as he reached his early nineties, but we were unable to convince him to move to the Kansas City area to be closer to us. Finally, at age 94, he agreed to move on one condition: He planned to spend several months in Israel, and I had to promise to present him with no obstacles. After extensive research, he found an acceptable senior residence near Jerusalem. Dave and I traveled with him and remained in Israel for a few days to make sure there were no problems. We need not have been concerned. Everything went smoothly. Bela lived in Israel as the Israelis do. His Hebrew improved, he made new friends, visited with old ones, and had a very brief taste of his lifelong dream of making aliyah. After three satisfying months, he was ready to come home. I went to meet him in Jerusalem, and we flew home together.

When the house on Donnybrook Drive was sold, my father relocated to Grand Court, a senior residential community in Overland Park, Kansas. Wanting to live in a Jewish environment, he moved again three years later to Village Shalom. His first two years there were pleasant. He enjoyed the Jewish aspects, along with all else it offered: lectures, various programs, the camaraderie of like-minded people, and the swimming pool. Subsequently, age-related problems began to limit his activities. He suffered from extensive hearing loss, and macular degeneration prevented him from doing what he loved best: reading. To assist with reading, he purchased a closed-circuit TV with a projection screen. The device was functional, but the required magnification limited projection of only one or two words at a time on the screen. Frustrated by this technology, my father put the device in a closet.

A more successful endeavor involved Tzivia Gaba, a family friend who had been a Hebrew and Judaic teacher in her working years. Tzivia visited my father about three times a week, sometimes more often. She regularly read to him, and together they studied history and the weekly Torah portion. My father and Tzivia both enjoyed their sessions together and became great friends.

Nearing centenarian status, Father's health began a precipitous decline, and he lost the will to live. We planned a 100th birthday party for him in November of 2003, but unfortunately he did not make it. He died October 31, 2003, just three and a half weeks before his 100th birthday.

My parents are both buried in Judean Gardens in Olney, Maryland.

Dave and I were both retired by the mid-1990s and began to embrace new phases of our lives. With more free time, I became a frequent Holocaust speaker and delivered dozens of lectures over a period of years. These activities highlighted the urgency of Holocaust testimonies as well as my desire to illuminate the atrocities committed. In-depth preparation for these presentations involved revisiting painful memories, at the same time making me appreciate how fortunate I was to be alive and able to provide such testimony.

Around this time, my father and I donated some artifacts to the US Holocaust Memorial Museum. While they can be seen on the museum's website, they have not been publicly displayed in the museum itself. Those artifacts were then discovered by the government of Lower Saxony in Germany that had built a museum and memorial at the site of the former Bergen-Belsen concentration camp. They borrowed the artifacts to be put on display there. In return, in 2007 they invited me and Dave as their guests at the memorial's dedication. At first I refused even to think about going to Germany; memories of the Nazi era had lingered, and I wanted to avoid all contact.

After weeks of contemplation, I changed my mind. The Nazis had tried to annihilate all of European Jewry, including my immediate family of three. Not only had my parents and I survived, but our family had grown and thrived. By 2007 we had four children, two daughters-in-law, and four grandchildren. Instead of three survivors, we were now a family of 11. I concluded that taking our entire family to the Bergen-Belsen dedication would make a statement, evidence of survival in spite of the Nazis' atrocities. And so all of our children, Cori, a daughter-in-law, and Annie, our only granddaughter at the time, accompanied Dave and me to Germany, making eight members of the Gondos-Jacobs family to attend the dedication.

Our family was assigned a car and driver for the duration of the visit. We learned on the second day that our driver was a volunteer who had donated his services and the use of his own vehicle to accommodate those his country had wronged. That one individual's efforts of recognition and reconciliation were much appreciated.

The two days we spent at the Bergen-Belsen site are a complete blur, though a few events are indelibly etched in memory. The camp itself had been liberated by the British, who then razed it because of a typhus epidemic. There was nothing left of the concentration camp our family had endured. I met dozens of Bergen-Belsen survivors and some of the Kasztner Train group. These meetings broadened my perspective. I acknowledged the existence of dozens of Kasztner Train survivors and realized that many had had postwar experiences similar to mine, in adapting to new cultures and living with lingering side effects.

There were sad memories of the 2007 trip, too. These include a visit to Anne Frank's grave, a child barely older than I in the 1940s, who did not survive. We also paid tribute at the site of mass graves. There are many of them, and each mound has a stone marker noting the deaths of the hundreds of souls buried beneath. But the grave markers contained only the number of deceased buried underneath, their individual names buried with them and lost forever.

I had many questions but few answers.

A group of survivors spontaneously walked to the original memorial established shortly after the war's end. There the group recited Kaddish, the memorial prayer for the dead. This brought tears to all eyes. There was another element to this Kaddish: Several elderly Germans, apparently not part of the survivor group and most likely not Jewish, also walked to the memorial. They stood in a small, separate group as we said Kaddish. Two of the men were sobbing as we turned back to the camp. We'll never know the reason, but I'd like to think it may have been sadness, guilt, or both.

A formal banquet was the culminating event of the dedication, a large affair to which many local and possibly national dignitaries had been invited. The aesthetics and the food were beyond reproach. A number of speeches followed food service. Headphones with a variety of translations were available, and I listened in Hungarian.

Several Holocaust survivors spoke, all with touching accounts of their experiences in Bergen-Belsen and their long-term consequences. A number of the German dignitaries also made presentations. My daughter, Diane, observed that their comments sounded like those at a dedication for a bridge or a building. We heard no apologies for the guilt of their forebearers. In their defense, they were dedicating a museum and memorial to past atrocities, so perhaps they felt that was enough.

The trip to Germany jolted me. Even though reliving Bergen-Belsen experiences was painful, I acknowledged gratitude for survival and the ability to live the life I chose. I realized that remembering the Holocaust is important, but learning and teaching its lessons is essential. How could another such catastrophe be prevented—or could it?

Back home, retirement continued to be better than we had hoped. Dave and I were free to do as we wished, and we continued to enjoy ourselves. Summer reunions for the entire family at the lake never disappointed anyone. Our numbers had increased, and we often needed to rent two additional condos to accommodate the group.

Added benefits included having the time to travel. We became avid snorkelers and enjoyed trips to the Great Barrier Reef,

French Polynesia, the Fiji Islands, and Hawaii. My father hosted us at Jasper Park Lodge in the Canadian Rockies, and later we were his guests in Israel and Jordan. My father observed that in his youth he had no money and in middle age he had no time—and in post-retirement, in his 80s and 90s, he had both time and money, but my mother was gone, and age had severely curtailed his ability to travel. These observations inspired us to continue smelling the roses while we were still able to.

We began to take cruises as Dave's mobility and energy declined. Ships took us to the British Isles, the Mediterranean, and all over the Caribbean. The kids enthusiastically joined us on an Alaskan cruise and one in Canada the following year. The children and grandchildren visited more often than they had in the past and were a source of joy to us both. We realized how fortunate we were to have raised such a wonderful family. And in one particular instance, wonderfully sneaky.

Every year, the UMKC Alumni Association presents a Defying the Odds Award to a UMKC graduate. A member of the search committee—one of my son Tom's professional contacts—had seen an article about me in the *Kansas City Star* and contacted Tom for further information. Unbeknownst to me, Tom and Jonathan were invited to present my case to the selection committee. They were asked to secure two letters of recommendation as well. Dave, Diane, and Dan all claimed to have been unaware of my candidacy.

One day, the phone rang. Immersed in a pension investment issue, I did not want to be disturbed and hoped the phone would stop ringing. It did not, and I answered it just before the call went to voicemail. The caller identified himself as Curt Crespino, vice chancellor of External Relations and Constituent Affairs at the University of Missouri–Kansas City. I assumed he was a fundraiser and immediately responded with my reasons for offering a very nominal donation.

Mr. Crespino politely listened until I had finished and then informed me that the UMKC Alumni Association had selected me to receive the 2016 Defying the Odds Award. The Bloch School of Management, which had awarded my MBA degree in 1977, and the School of Education, where I received my PhD in higher educational administration in 1986, had both sponsored my candidacy.

Realizing this was not a fundraising call, I assumed it had to be a prank and expressed that sentiment to Mr. Crespino. Very calmly, he asked me to contact the individual in charge of alumni awards and provided her phone number. Still suspicious, rather than use the number he had given me, I called the university switchboard to contact her. Much to my surprise, Mr. Crespino's call had been legitimate.

Preparations for the ceremony were all-encompassing. They included a photographic session for publicity, with wardrobe suggestions. There were multiple interviews. Lunch with the dean of the Bloch School provided opportunity to learn about exciting changes in the MBA program. UMKC Chancellor Leo Morton hosted a cocktail reception where he presented each honoree with a signed Tom Curran-commissioned bronze kangaroo, the UMKC mascot. Ten-foot-tall pictures of the honorees adorned the party room.

The awards ceremony, a luncheon, took place on April 21, 2016, one week before my 79th birthday. I received two standing ovations—the only two that day. Administrators of the Henry Bloch School of Management had invited me to make a Holocaust presentation shortly after the awards ceremony. There were several hundred attendees. The audience was receptive and engaged. The following week, I spoke to graduate students and faculty at the School of Education. It, too, was a gratifying experience.

We shared pride in our children, a sentiment Dave frequently verbalized during his later years. It recalled a time sitting in my parents' living room in the early 1960s, where a friend of my mother's said, "Ilona, you've raised such a wonderful daughter." Smiling, my mother replied, "Not wonderful because of me, but in spite of me." Just as my mother had expressed, I deserve little credit for my four wonderful children, but my joy in them is immeasurable. They are the true source of my "nachas"—Yiddish for pride and joy.

Diane, Dan, Tom, and Jonathan are all successful, living satisfying lives. As busy as they are, they have embraced the values Dave and I shared. I'm particularly grateful that their personal achievements have not dimmed their interest in education about the Holocaust and its widespread implications.

Sadly, Dave's physical condition continued to deteriorate over the course of the next few years. It became terminal during the peak of the pandemic, yet more than once our children and grandchildren drove thousands of miles to spend time with him. They were all there when he died September 13, 2020, at the age of 88. He was buried at Mt. Carmel Cemetery in Kansas City, Missouri. The family made meaningful comments at the funeral as well as at the unveiling, when we set the stone marker. An impromptu thought crossed my mind during the unveiling, and I shared it with the family: I was grateful that we were able to share happy memories. And unlike the thousands of Holocaust victims lying in mass graves in Bergen-Belsen or my grandparents, whose lives had been terminated at Auschwitz, Dave had his own individual grave marker.

After Dave's death, I was alone for the first time in 63 years. The pandemic had isolated me, and I no longer enjoyed the large house we had shared for decades. Continuing to live in Wycklow was no longer a viable option. Fortunately the house sold in one day. Selling was the easy part. Where to move next proved to be more difficult. I ultimately decided to move to Village Shalom.

Village Shalom describes itself as a community, but I gave that aspect very little consideration, and initially I did not think about interactions with future neighbors. I just wanted a place to live in my own space.

My prior communal living experiences had been limited to a year in boarding school, one summer at camp, and five semesters in the University of Michigan residence halls. I had much in common with fellow students enrolled at boarding school in Switzerland, as many were refugees like me. At Jewish camp, we shared a common commitment to Judaism. The Ann Arbor dorms, all single-sex at the time, housed a varied group of women—rich and poor, socially adept and reclusive, Easterners, Westerners, Midwesterners, foreigners, Jews and Christians—and we were there for the same reason: to learn. But in the move to Village Shalom, I was not really thinking of communal purpose.

The advantages of community that exist at Village Shalom did not become apparent until after I moved here in April of 2021. As a residential community for seniors, Village Shalom provides opportunities for residents to optimize life experiences in the present. Living in the present makes sense, and much to my surprise, there are residents with whom I have discovered mutual interests.

Some communal living aspects have been unexpected. Being a very private person, I've never offered more information about myself than necessary. It has been surprising to find that people often know more about me than I have personally disclosed and that inadvertently, I have information about others I would just as soon not know.

In a sense, I've had to reinvent myself: a new phase of my life, where I've defined new parameters. In my new surroundings I am known as Judy. My long-standing identity as Judith G. Jacobs, PhD, Mrs. David Jacobs, or the mother of Diane, Dan, Tom, and Jonathan is not erased but is no longer dominant. I recently talked to Jonathan about the "reinvented" me, and his response was, "Isn't that good, Mom?" I guess it is. I'm a new Judy.

Taking the opportunities afforded to me to speak at schools, colleges, and community groups offers a living history lesson to many on the horrors of the past, in the hope of preventing such atrocities in the future. Learning the lessons of the past can inform us about the depths to which human beings are able to sink to achieve their ends.

Could there be another Holocaust? Yes. The widespread presence of hate, anger, and intolerance today provides a ripe environment for destruction on the same or similar scale. Can we prevent another Holocaust? I hope so. Teaching about other peoples and their cultures and emphasizing tolerance, understanding, and kindness could go a long way toward promoting a hate-free society. Love, not hate. Acceptance, never genocide.

The Final Word

The title of this chapter originated with my father. He had delivered numerous Holocaust-related lectures and written many papers on the subject. He hoped to write a book, most likely a memoir, entitled *The Final Word*. Although he was highly productive throughout his life, the plan for his book was conceived too late in life and did not materialize. I dedicate "The Final Word" to my father, Bela, and my mother, Anna Ilona, my father's source of support and inspiration. "Zichronam livrach," Hebrew for "may their memories be a blessing."

I was born into a loving home in Budapest, and my early childhood was unparalleled with doting parents and grandparents. Then we lived through hell. My father and mother were the kinds of parents everyone hopes to have. They consistently sheltered, loved, and supported me. Even during the darkest days, they engaged in constructive activities providing me with a glimmer of hope for a better tomorrow. We came to a new land and seized the opportunity to pursue our goals. Through relentless effort Mother and Father rebuilt their shattered lives and laid the foundation for my future.

Loyal American citizens for decades, my parents continued to feel like transplants in this country. There was much in American culture they did not understand and many nuances in the English language they were unable to master. Even here decades later, when he felt sentimental, my father called me Jutka.

The Nazis murdered 6,000,000 of our people, including most of my extended family. The broken family chain left a chasm in our lives. Diane, Dan, Tom, and Jonathan benefitted from the love and wisdom of wonderful grandparents. I missed most of that opportunity. My parents were a source of love, support, advice, and friendship during my adult years, but the Nazis deprived them of such an experience with their own parents.

Thanks to my marriage to David Jacobs, a Midwesterner, raising four children in Kansas, and benefitting from an American education, I can confidently say that I have mostly assimilated to American culture. Even so, I recognize that the Holocaust has left a discernible gap in my childhood development.

My formative years were spent trying to survive, and I had little opportunity to play. I still don't know how to ride a bike. I avoid trains due to lifelong psychological trauma from the train ride to hell. The sound of marching boots hitting the ground continues to send shivers down my spine.

Necessity turned me into a loner when I was a youngster. Life changed fast, and outcomes were unpredictable. It was neither safe to trust others nor to form strong relationships.

THE FINAL WORD

The value and portability of my father's knowledge and career strongly impressed me early in life. It enabled him to pursue the profession he loved in the United States and led me to recognize the importance of education. It also accounts for my drive to excel.

But most importantly, Hitler's attempts to eradicate our Jewish family did not succeed. We started as a nuclear family of three, and currently we number 21.

Living through the Shoah formed much of who I am and will undoubtedly influence my children, grandchildren, and even great-grandchildren. I hope they will remember and learn its lessons. There are many questions but few answers.

While my personal loss is palpable, I speak out today, relaying my experiences to broaden the circle of those able to recognize such heinous inhumanity should they, God forbid, encounter it. Atrocities that have happened are atrocities that may still happen and can still happen. My hope is that telling what I know to people willing to listen can be something positive—increasing, however slightly, the number of those willing to rise up to stop it.

With the support of my family, my parents in the early years, David for 63 years, my children and grandchildren, I've reached some meaningful personal goals, including the MBA and the PhD. However, in the final "cheshbon"—Hebrew for bill or accounting—I sum it all up differently: My life's greatest achievements include being a wife, mother, grandmother, and now a great-grandmother.

APPENDIX

◆

Family Photos

Wedding portrait of Mor and Roza Gondos,
Erdőbénye, Hungary, about 1898.

JUTKA

Portraits of Mor and Roza Gondos taken in early twentieth century.

The Gondos family, portrait taken in Sátoraljaújhely, Hungary, early twentieth century.
Top row, left to right: Sanyi, Zelma, Sarolta, Ilonka, Bela
Front row, left to right: Mor, Roza, Zoli

FAMILY PHOTOS

Ilona and her brother, Laci, taken in Békés, Hungary, about 1924.

Ilona and Bela in Budapest, around 1931.

JUTKA

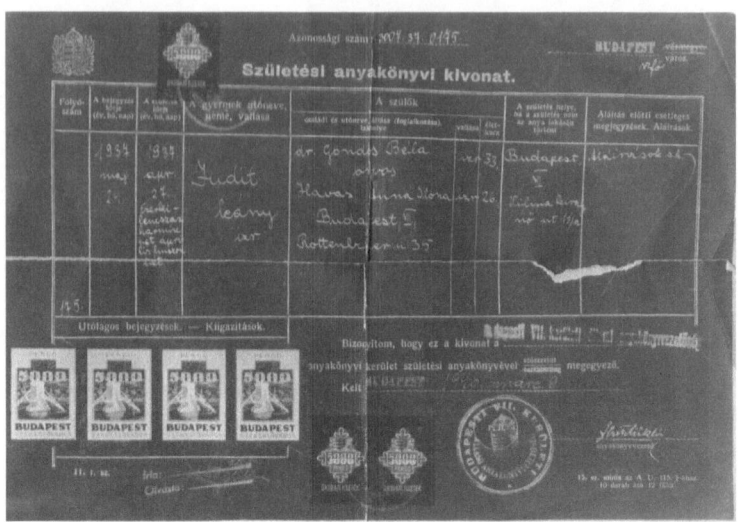

Judit Gondos's birth certificate.

Rottenbilller utca 35, the apartment building in Budapest where Jutka, Ilona, and Bela lived.

FAMILY PHOTOS

Courtyard of the apartment building where the Gondos family lived in Budapest.

The Havas family home in Békés, Hungary.

JUTKA

Jutka and Jakab Havas, Békés, Hungary, around 1938.

Iren and Jutka in Békés, Hungary, around 1938.

FAMILY PHOTOS

Ilona (standing), Jutka (in swing), and Eva (cousin; standing right), Békés, Hungary, around 1938.

Iren and Jakab in their home in Békés, Hungary, around 1939.

JUTKA

Jutka and Bela ice-skating in Budapest, about 1941.

The Gondos family in Budapest, Hungary, portrait taken in the late 1930s.
Top row, left to right: Bela, Ilona, Margaret, Zoli, Margalit, Sanyi
Front row, left to right: Zelma, Roza, Ilonka, Lili

FAMILY PHOTOS

The extended Havas family in Békés, Hungary, around 1942.
Top row, left to right: Pircsi, Jakab
Bottom row, left to right: Iren, Jutka, Eva

Gondos family in Mezőkövesd, Hungary, picture taken around 1942.
Top row, left to right: Peter, Bandi
Bottom row, left to right: Jutka, Roza, Tomi

JUTKA

Nomi Gondos, family friend, and Jutka in Budapest, Hungary, around 1942.

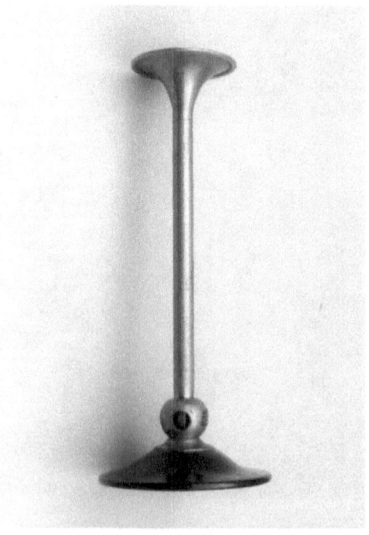

Bela Gondos's medical school stethoscope. It was used in Bergen-Belsen and accompanied the family to Switzerland and then to the United States.

FAMILY PHOTOS

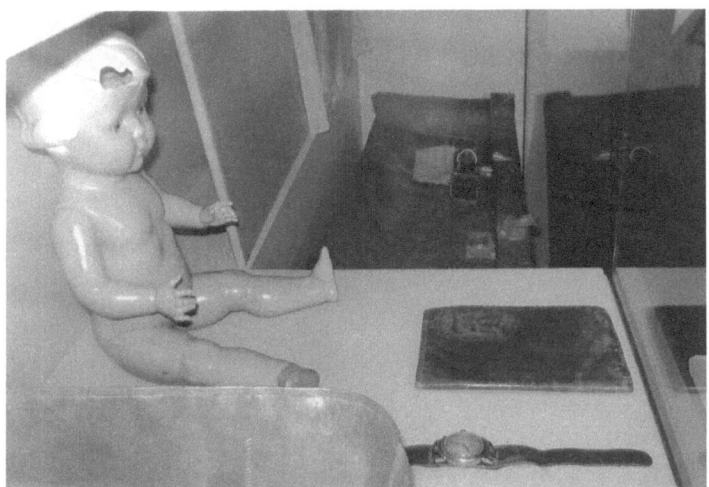

Gondos family objects that accompanied them to the Bergen-Belsen concentration camp: aluminum picnic box, Jutka's doll, Bela's watch, passport case, and large suitcase. Donated to the US Holocaust Memorial Museum, Washington, DC.

Ilona, Bela, and Juka in Switzerland, about 1945.

Ilona, Jutka, and Bela, in Switzerland, spring 1946.

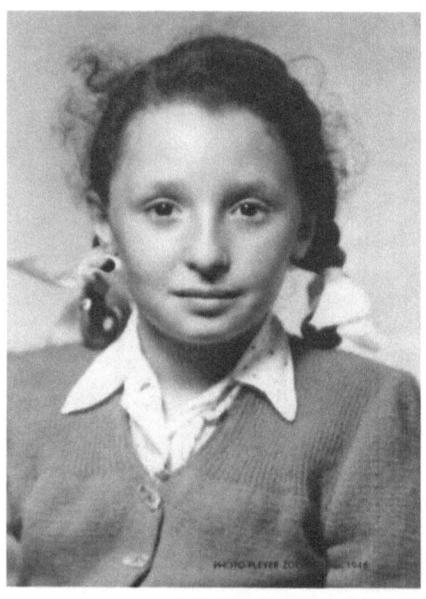

Jutka in Switzerland, 1946.

FAMILY PHOTOS

Margaret and Gordon Gondos in Arlington, Virginia, about 1945.

Judy and David at Alice Lloyd formal dance at
the University of Michigan, January, 1957.

JUTKA

Ilona and Judy in Chevy Chase, Maryland, August, 1957.

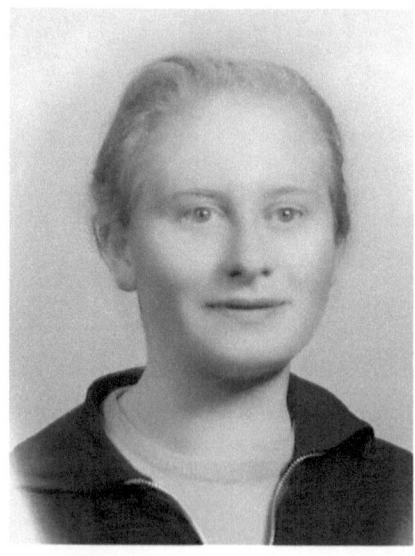

Nomi Gondos, portrait in Israel. Early 1960s.

FAMILY PHOTOS

Ilona and Bela on front porch of their home in Chevy Chase, Maryland.

Ilona and Bela, on vacation, 1970s.

The Jacobs home for 25 years. It burned in 1991.

The extended Jacobs family at their Lake of the Ozarks home around 1984.
Back row, left to right: David, Judy, Diane, Tom
Front row, left to right: Jonathan, Bela, Ilona, Dan

FAMILY PHOTOS

Members of Gondos-Jacobs family in Baltimore, 1988.
Back row, left to right: Gordon, Myra, Brian, Zoltan, Judy
Front row, left to right: Gary, Bela, Jonathan

Bela and his brother, Zoltan, in Chevy Chase, Maryland, 1993.

The extended Jacobs family at Cape Canaveral Beach, Florida, about 2010.
Front to back: Ezra, Rachel, Forrest, Avi, Eli
Back row, left to right: Judy, Annie, Max, David
Back row: Ariel

The Jacobs extended family visiting Bergen-Belsen memorial and museum, around 2014.
Back row, left to right: Tom, Jonathan, Cori
Front row, left to right: David, Judy, Dan, Diane, Annie

FAMILY PHOTOS

Judy Jacobs featured in *UMKC Today* magazine. "Surviving the Holocaust," *UMKC Today*, University of Missouri–Kansas City, February 26, 2016.

The extended Jacobs Family at Defying the Odds Award ceremony, University of Missouri-Kansas City, 2016.
Back row, left to right: Tom, Sherri, David, Eli, Dan, Cori, Diane, Barb
Front row, left to right: Forrest, Judy, Ezra, Rachel

The extended Jacobs family in Denali National Park, Alaska, around 2017.
Back row, left to right: David, Judy, Annie, friend Monica, Jonathan
Front row, left to right: Rachel, Ezra

The extended Jacobs family at a hot air balloon festival in New Mexico, in 2017.

FAMILY PHOTOS

The extended Jacobs family on a Caribbean cruise in 2022.
Back row, left to right: Tom, Ezra, Eli, Forrest
Middle row, left to right: Cori, Diane, Judy, Ariel, Rachel, Dan, Max, Gillian
Front row, seated, left to right: Jonathan, Sherri, Simcha, Shira

Family Genealogy

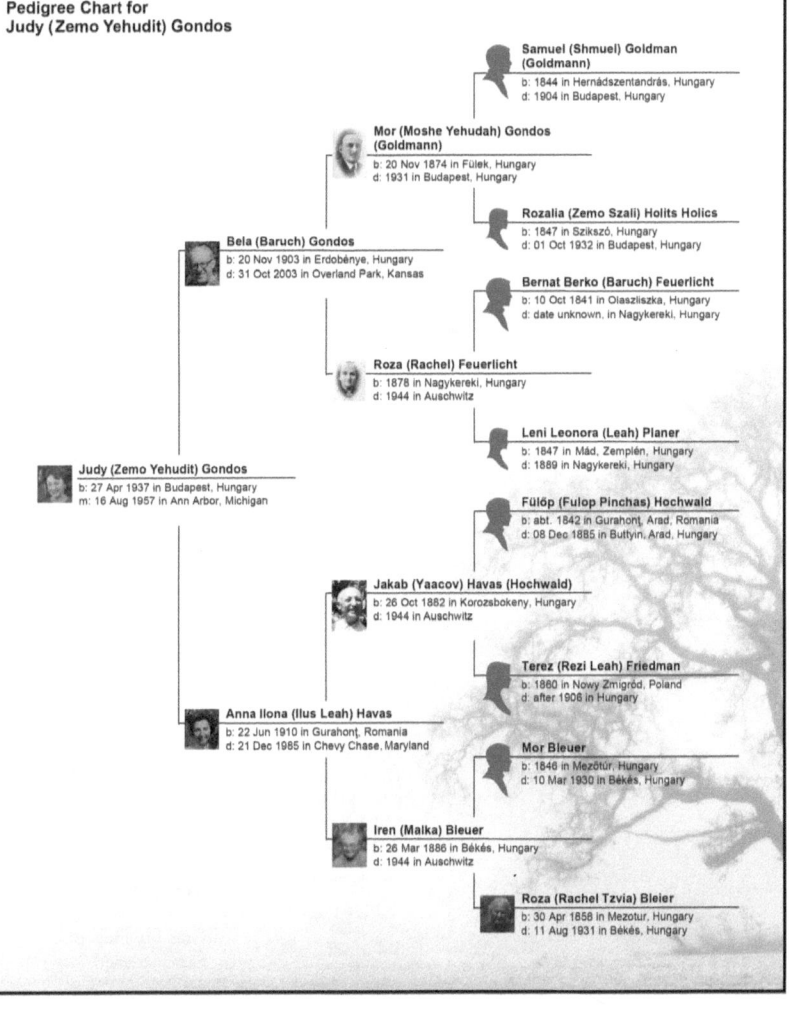

JUTKA

Kinship Report

LAST NAME	FIRST NAME	BIRTH YEAR	RELATIONSHIP	RELATIVES
Adler	Andras (Bandi)	1933	Paternal 1st cousin	Son of Bela's sister Zelma
Adler	Lajos	1902	Husband of aunt	Married to Bela's sister Zelma
Adler	Peter (Peti)	1935	Paternal 1st cousin	Son of Bela's sister Zelma
Adler	Tamas (Tomi)	~ 1937	Paternal 1st cousin	Son of Bela's sister Zelma
Baill	Cori (Chaya)	1956	Daughter-in-law	Married to Daniel Jacobs
Bialer	Gillian A	1988	Mother of great-grandson	Mother of Samuel Jacobs
Biro	Eva	~ 1930	1st cousin 1x removed	Daughter of Emil Biro (maternal grandmother's brother)
Biro (born Bleuer)	Emil	1891	Great-uncle	Brother of maternal grandmother
Biro (born Bleuer)	Erno	1889	Great-uncle	Brother of maternal grandmother
Bleier	Roza (Rachel Tzvia)	1858	Great-grandmother	Mother of maternal grandmother
Bleier	Salamon (Shalom Shloma)	~ 1833	2nd great-grandfather	On my mother's mother's side
Braun	Myra	1947	Married to cousin Gordon Gondos	
Brudoley	Abraham Samson (Avraham) (Avi)	2001	Stepson of son Jonathan	
Brudoley	Ariel Aron	1999	Stepson of son Jonathan	
Brudoley	Simcha Zev	2021	Step-grandchild	Son of Ariel Brudoley
Brudoley	Tova Yael	2023	Step-granddaughter	Daughter of Ariel Brudoley
Conn (Kohn)	Alexander (Sandor)	1904	1st cousin 2x removed	Son of Matilda Bleier, my great-grandmother's sister
Eubanks	Michael	1989	Husband of granddaughter Anna Ilona Jacobs	
Farkas	Andrew A (András)	1945	Husband of 3rd cousin	Judith Wohl (a Planer)
Farkas	Judy	unknown	3rd cousin	Granddaughter of Sarolta Planer

FAMILY GENEALOGY

LAST NAME	FIRST NAME	BIRTH YEAR	RELATIONSHIP	RELATIVES
Feuerlicht	Berko (Baruch)	~1795	3rd great-grandfather (there were 2 Baruch Feuerlichts)	
Feuerlicht	Bernat (Baruch)	1841	Great-grandfather (there were 2 Baruch Feuerlichts)	
Feuerlicht	Jozsef (Josef)	1820	2nd great-grandfather	
Feuerlicht	Roza (Rachel)	1878	Paternal grandmother	
Feuerlicht	Sarolta	1883	Great-aunt	Sister of grandmother, Rosa Feuerlicht; lived with Bela's family
Fisch	Margaret (Margret)	1912	Wife of uncle Zoltan Gondos	
Friedman	Terez (Rezi Leah)	1860	Great-grandmother	Married to Fulop Hochwald
Galla	Éva Zsuzsanna (Zsuzsi)	1917	1st cousin 1x removed	Daughter of Bela's uncle Beno Galla
Galla	János Ivan (Jancsi)	1928	1st cousin 1x removed	Son of Bela's uncle Beno Galla
Galla	Péter	1967	2nd cousin	Son of Janos Galla
Galla (Goldmann)	Beno (Beno)	1888	Great-uncle	Brother of Mor
Galla (Goldmann)	Thomas (Tamás)	1923	1st cousin 1x removed	Son of Beno Galla
Goldmann	Mor (Moshe)	~1822	2nd great-grandfather (there were 2 Mor Goldmanns, the 2nd changed his name to Gondos)	
Gondos	Brian Kenneth (Paltiel Mordechai)	1976	1st cousin 1x removed	Son of cousin Gordon Gondos
Gondos	Erzsébet (Erzsebet Erzsi)	1911	1st cousin 1x removed	Daughter of Mor's brother Bernat
Gondos	Gary J (Zvi Yeremiyahu Eliezer—maternal and paternal grandfathers)	1971	1st cousin 1x removed	Son of my cousin Gordon Gondos

JUTKA

LAST NAME	FIRST NAME	BIRTH YEAR	RELATIONSHIP	RELATIVES
Gondos	Gordon Morris Benjamin (Moshe Yehudah)	1944	Paternal 1st cousin	Son of Bela's brother, Zoltan
Gondos	Henrik	1910	1st cousin 1x removed	Son of Mor's brother Vilmos (Villi baci) Gondos
Gondos	Klara Klari	~1912	1st cousin 1x removed	Daughter of Mor's brother Bernat (Berci baci) Gondos
Gondos	Nomi (Katalin Kati)	1939	Paternal 1st cousin	Daughter of Bela's brother, Sanyi
Gondos	Sandor (Sanyi)	1906	Uncle	Bela's brother
Gondos	Zoltan (Yosef Zelig)	1908	Uncle	Bela's brother
Gondos (born Goldmann)	Bela (Baruch)	1903	Father	
Gondos (born Goldmann)	Bernát (Bernat Berci)	1882	Great-uncle	
Gondos (born Goldmann)	Ilona (Ilonka)	1900	Aunt	
Gondos (born Goldmann)	Mor (Moshe Yehudah)	1874	Paternal grandfather	
Gondos (born Goldmann)	Vilmos (Villi)	~1872	Great-uncle	Mor's brother
Gondos (born Goldmann)	Zelma (Zelike Chaya Sara)	1902	Aunt	Bela's sister
Grunwald	Iren (Pircsi)	1911	Wife of uncle	Married to my mother's brother Imre Laszlo (Laci)
Havas	Anna Ilona (Ilus Leah)	1910	Mother	
Havas	Elizabeth (Erzsebet Ela)	1904	1st cousin 1x removed	Daughter of Jakab Havas' brother Adolf Hochwald
Havas	Esther (Iren)	1900	1st cousin 1x removed	Daughter of Jakab Havas' brother Herman Hochwald
Havas	Imre Laszlo (Laci Pinchas)	1908	Uncle	My mother's brother
Havas (Hochwald)	Jakab (Yaacov)	1882	Maternal grandfather	
Hochwald	Adolf (Avraham)	~1880	Great-uncle	Brother of my grandfather, Jakab Havas

FAMILY GENEALOGY

LAST NAME	FIRST NAME	BIRTH YEAR	RELATIONSHIP	RELATIVES
Hochwald	Fülop (Fulop Pinchas)	~1842	Great-grandfather	
Hochwald	Gisella Gisa	unknown	1st cousin 1x removed	Daughter of Jakab Havas' brother Herman Hochwald
Hochwald	Herman	1884	Great-uncle	Brother of Jakab Havas
Hochwald	Magdalena (Malka)	1914	1st cousin 1x removed	Daughter of Jakab Havas' brother Herman Hochwald
Hochwald	Mari (Maria)	1859	Great-aunt	Sister of Jakab Havas
Hochwald	Sandor (Noni)	~1904	1st cousin 1x removed	Son of Jakab Havas' brother Herman Hochwald
Holczer	Ilona (Ilka)	1902	Wife of 1st great-uncle	Married to my grandmother's brother, Emil Biro
Holits Holics	Rozalia (Zemo Szali)	1847	Great-grandmother	Married to Samuel Goldmann and mother of Mor Gondos
Jacobs	Daniel Harry (Tzvi)	1961	Son	
Jacobs	David Samuel (David)	1931	Husband	
Jacobs	Diane S (Rachel Malka)	1958	Daughter	
Jacobs	Ezra Samuel	2008	Grandson	Son of Jonathan
Jacobs	Forrest Bernard (Baruch Dov)	2004	Grandson	Son of Thomas
Jacobs	Jonathan Todd (Avraham Pinchas)	1968	Son	
Jacobs	Jordan Max Baill (Ariel)	1989	Grandson	Son of Daniel
Jacobs	Judy (Zemo Yehudit) Gondos	1937	Self	
Jacobs	Rachel Ilona (Rachel)	2008	Granddaughter	Daughter of Jonathan
Jacobs	Samuel Francis Bialer (Shmuel)	2023	Great-grandson	Son of Jordan

JUTKA

LAST NAME	FIRST NAME	BIRTH YEAR	RELATIONSHIP	RELATIVES
Jacobs	Thomas Dale (Tom) (Moshe Yaakov)	1964	Son	
Klezer	Sali	~ 1826	2nd great-grandmother	Married to Szigmond Planer
Kohn	Piroska (Piri)	~ 1897	1st cousin 2x removed	Daughter of Alexander/Sandor Kohn (a Bleier)
Kövesi	Margalit (Margit Manci)	1908	Wife of uncle	Married to Sanyi Gondos
Kusnetz	Shira Chana	1999	Wife of stepson of son	Married to Ariel Brudoley
Martosh (Martos Eisenberger Eisenberg)	Andrew (Endre) (Yisroel) (Ocsi)	1925	2nd cousin (a Feuerlicht)	
Planer	Szigmond (Yehoshua Asher Zelig) [Sigmond]	1815	2nd great-grandfather	Father of Leah Feuerlicht
Pollak	Gabriella (Gabi)	~ 1960	2nd cousin 1x removed	Great-granddaughter of Jakab Havas' brother Herman Hochwald
Rechnitz	Eugene (Jeno)	unknown	Husband of aunt	Married to Bela's sister Ilona Gondos
Rechnitz	Lidia (Lili)	~ 1925	Paternal 1st cousin	Daughter of Bela's sister Ilona
Roth	Julia (Jetti Julie)	~ 1820	2nd great-grandmother	Married to Jozsef Feuerlicht
Siegler	Jolan	1884	Wife of great-uncle	Married to Mor's brother Bernat Gondos
Székely (Szekely)	Tamás (Tamas Tami)	1942	2nd cousin	Son of Erzsi Gondos
Walther	Eli Roger Jacobs	2002	Grandson	Son of Diane
Walther	Jeffrey Dale	1963	Father of grandson Eli Walther	
Wishnow	Barbara Rae	1963	Daughter-in-law	Mother of Forrest

Family Members Lost to the Holocaust

These are some of the family members we lost in the Holocaust:

Gondos, close family (my father's family):

- Rosa (Rachel) Feuerlicht Gondos, my grandmother. Diane's Hebrew name is for hers.
- Zelma Gondos Adler, my aunt
- Peter Adler, my first cousin
- Andras (Bandi) Adler, my first cousin
- Tamas (Tami) Adler, my first cousin
- Ilona (Ilonka) Gondos Rechnitz, my aunt
- Lidia (Lili) Rechnitz, my first cousin

JUTKA

Havas, close family
(my mother's family):

- Jakab Havas, my grandfather
- Iren (Malka) Bleuer Havas, my grandmother. Diane's Hebrew name is for hers.
- Imre Laszlo (Laci, Pinchas) Havas, my uncle. Tom's Hebrew name is for his.
- Iren (Pircsi) Grunwald Havas, Laci's wife

Havas, extended family:

We are unaware of any Havas family who died in the Shoah, other than my grandfather.

Bleuer/Bleier, extended family
(my grandmother Havas' family):

- Iren Bleuer Havas, my grandmother
- Sandor Biro (born Bleuer), my grandmother's brother
- Jolan Bleuer, my grandmother's sister
- Terez Bleuer, my grandmother's sister
- Saul/Salamon/Sali Biro (born Bleuer), my grandmother's brother
- Erno Biro (born Bleuer), my grandmother's brother. Died shortly after the Shoah.
- Emil Biro (born Bleuer), my grandmother's brother.
- Sandor Biro's wife, Ilona Rasovitz

FAMILY MEMBERS LOST TO THE HOLOCAUST

- Sandor Biro's son, Bela Biro (unsure of this one)
- Sandor Biro's daughter, Anna Biro (unsure)
- Emil Biro, my grandmother's brother
- Ilona Holczer, Emil's wife
- Eva Biro, Emil's daughter

Gondos/Goldmann, extended family (my father's family):

- Vilmos (Vili) Gondos, my grandfather's brother
- Villi's wife, Berta
- Villi's son, Henrik
- Bernat (Berci) Gondos, my grandfather's brother

Feuerlicht extended family (my paternal grandmother's family):

- Sarolta Feuerlicht, my grandmother's sister, who lived with my dad's family
- Szali Feuerlicht, my grandmother's sister
- Lena Feuerlicht, my grandmother's sister
- Lipot Feuerlicht, my grandmother's brother
- Sarolta Berger Feuerlicht, Lipot's wife
- Zoltan Feuerlicht, my grandmother's brother
- Bela Feuerlicht, my grandmother's brother

JUTKA

Planer extended family (my paternal great-grandmother's family):

- Bernat (Dov Beer) Planer, my grandmother's first cousin
- Szeren Planer Moscovics, Bernat's daughter
- Rosika Planer, my grandmother's first cousin once removed
- Zelig (Zsiga) Planer, my grandmother's cousin once removed
- Betti Planer Reisner, my grandmother's cousin once removed
- Sandor Reisner, my grandmother's cousin once removed
- Joseph Fried, my grandmother's cousin once removed
- Erzsi Fried, my grandmother's cousin once removed
- Zsigmond Planer (a different Zsigmond Planer), my grandmother's cousin once removed
- Mina Mindel Hollaner Planer, wife of Zsigmond
- Vera (Perl) Planer, Zsigmond's daughter
- Reizl Planer, Zsigmond's daughter
- Braindel Planer, Zsigmond's daughter
- Sara Planer, Zsigmond's daughter
- Tzvi Planer, Zsigmond's son
- Dov Planer, Zsigmond's son
- Herman (Hirsch Tzvi) Planer, my grandmother's first cousin
- Shmuel Planer, Herman's son
- Vilmos Planre, Herman's son
- Zsigmond Planer, Herman's son

FAMILY MEMBERS LOST TO THE HOLOCAUST

- Bernhard Planer, my grandmother's uncle
- Sali Sarah Planer, Bernhard's daughter
- Joseph Planer, Bernhard's son
- Zsigmond (another Zsigmond) Planer, Bernhard's son
- Simon Planre, Bernhard's son
- Iren Planer, Bernhard's daughter
- Mor Planer, my grandmother's uncle
- Lina Feldman Planer, Mor's wife
- Iren Planer Fried, Mor's daughter
- Kornelia Chava Planer Kolchier, Mor's daughter
- Tibor Kolchier, Kornelia's son
- Jeno Kolchier, Kornelia's son
- Miklos Kolchier, Kornelia's son
- Jeruchem Kolchier, Kornelia's son
- Adolf/Abraham Planer, my grandmother's first cousin
- Izidor Planer, my grandmother's first cousin
- Zanwyl Planer, my grandmother's first cousin
- Dov Planer, my grandmother's first cousin

Acknowledgments

Recording early childhood Holocaust experiences forced me to relive some horrendous trauma. But, much to my surprise, I also recalled some happy times. I am grateful for the brief opportunity to smile.

This accounting could not have happened without the inspiration and help of my family. David, though not a Holocaust survivor, strongly urged me to share the horrors of my family's experiences and patiently encouraged me to keep on writing. Diane has been the soul of this project, encouraging me to meet the challenge when I had doubts, inspiring me with hope when I was overwhelmed, and doing whatever she could—whenever she could—to help me move forward. Ever ready to help but never intrusive, Cori provided excellent ideas early in the project and helped to bring this project to fruition. Dan, Tom, Jonathan, Sherri, and Barb all added their imprint—making useful suggestions, providing pertinent facts and details, proofreading, and giving me unending support and encouragement.

My eight grandchildren and three great-grandchildren provide testimony that the Nazis' attempt at annihilation of the Jews did not succeed. Our nuclear family of three—my parents and I—survived the Holocaust, and now we are a family of 21. The grandchildren have all shown interest in this turbulent part of our family's history. Max, Annie, Ariel, Avi, Eli, Forrest, Ezra, and Rachel have participated—each in their own way—in my efforts to teach about the Holocaust and its lessons.

I express appreciation to Michael Ashcraft for his invaluable help in organizing a series of memories and vignettes into a coherent whole and unjudgmentally editing where necessary.

My gratitude to the Greenleaf team, particularly to lead editor Lee Reed Zarnikau. Lee expertly and patiently helped me to navigate the maze of getting a book published. I thank Mimi Bark for her skillful designs and Brian Welch for ably managing the project.

About the Author

Judy Gondos Jacobs, survivor of the Holocaust, was born in Budapest, Hungary. Judy and her parents immigrated to the United States in 1946. She earned a BA at the University of Michigan in 1960 and MBA and PhD at the University of Missouri-Kansas City, in 1977 and 1986, respectively. Judy is the mother of four, grandmother of eight, and great-grandmother of three. Committed to teaching about the Holocaust and its lessons, Judy speaks frequently to a variety of groups. She lives in Overland Park, Kansas.

www.ingramcontent.com/pod-product-compliance
Lightning Source LLC
Chambersburg PA
CBHW030517080526
44586CB00011B/220